Language Choice and Identity Politics in Taiwan

Language Choice and Identity Politics in Taiwan

JENNIFER M. WEI

LEXINGTON BOOKS

A division of
ROWMAN & LITTLEFIELD PUBLISHERS, INC.
Lanham • Boulder • New York • Toronto • Plymouth, UK

LEXINGTON BOOKS

A division of Rowman & Littlefield Publishers, Inc.
A wholly owned subsidiary of The Rowman & Littlefield Publishing Group, Inc.
4501 Forbes Boulevard, Suite 200
Lanham, MD 20706

Estover Road
Plymouth PL6 7PY
United Kingdom

Copyright © 2008 by Lexington Books

All rights reserved. No part of this publication may be reproduced, stored in a retrieval system, or transmitted in any form or by any means, electronic, mechanical, photocopying, recording, or otherwise, without the prior permission of the publisher.

British Library Cataloguing in Publication Information Available

Library of Congress Cataloging-in-Publication Data

Wei, Jennifer M., 1964-
 Language choice and identity politics in Taiwan / Jennifer M. Wei.
   p. cm.
 Includes bibliographical references.
 ISBN-13: 978-0-7391-2352-2 (cloth : alk. paper)
 ISBN-10: 0-7391-2352-1 (cloth : alk. paper)
 1. Language awareness—Taiwan. 2. Identity (Psychology) 3. Taiwan—Languages—Political aspects. 4. Language policy—Taiwan. 5. Chinese language—Taiwan. I. Title.
 P120.L34W45 2008
 306.4'4951249—dc22

2007052944

Printed in the United States of America

♾™ The paper used in this publication meets the minimum requirements of American National Standard for Information Sciences—Permanence of Paper for Printed Library Materials, ANSI/NISO Z39.48-1992.

For Andrew

Contents

Preface		ix
Introduction		xv
Chapter 1	To –Er Is to Err: Acts of Identity in Chinese	1
Chapter 2	Language Choice in Mandarin and Tai-yu	19
Chapter 3	Chen Shui-bian's Language Choices	33
Chapter 4	Language Choice and Politics	35
Chapter 5	From Nationalism to Multiculturalism: Making Choices in Language Policy	81
Chapter 6	A Hybrid Chinese for the Twenty-first Century	103
Bibliography		121
Index		131
About the Author		133

Preface

I wish there had been a book on identity politics when I was growing up in Taipei during the late Kuomintang (KMT) era. Instead, I was assured of the importance of being Chinese and educated accordingly. It felt natural to me since I came from a military family, and referring to things Chinese was so familiar. China was my grandparents' homeland and Taiwan was a just a transitional stop. Coming to Taiwan was almost like a sojourn in the countryside, while the eventual return to China was everything to be serious about.

A book on identity politics would have been helpful to me when I was starting my career in Taipei in the early 1990s. A negation of everything Chinese was on its way in. Regimes changed. People were excited, enraged, overwrought. The pro-democracy student demonstrations in Beijing might have ended in 1989, but political rallies and protests of a party nature were unrelenting in Taipei.[1] Ways of being, speaking, and knowing all became divisive under the cover of democracy. Familiar figures revered in childhood were now treated as corrupt bureaucrats. Mandarin accented with flawless retroflexes was seen as the "dialect of Beijing." Names of streets and contexts of textbooks were changed to acknowledge ethnic and political injustice and make way for an increasingly diversified political scene. "Becoming Taiwanese" became not only a social condition but also a political one.

What I didn't realize in childhood and in formative youth, but either read or learned about later, was that Taiwan, like the rest of the world in the 1960s, was very much influenced by the Cold War. Yet, unlike the rest of the world, our preoccupation was not with the Korean War or Vietnam but with the Chinese Communist Party (CCP). The civil war between the KMT and the CCP in the 1940s had resulted in more than massive emigration of Chinese to Taiwan. Millions of military personnel and civilians fled, abandoning everything with the thought that they would be back and reunited with their parents, wives and children as soon as the war was over. The war persisted. The KMT lost not only the mainland to the CCP but also its legitimacy to represent China. In the 1970s a series of diplomatic setbacks in the UN and with the U.S. further isolated and devastated the KMT in Taiwan. Taiwan became a nation without a state, or a state whose definition and legitimacy is still in conflict with the CCP's One China policy.

Determination to rule and represent China, frustration with realities, and discontent among the Taiwanese people, whose experience with and expectations of government had been influenced by the Japanese during the Occupation (1895 to 1945), all contributed to the implementation of strong nationalism and patriotism. A tight control of all aspects of national machinery including the media and education helped shield the people from what was really going on in the world and raised a generation of Chinese whose cultural practices, national allegiance and linguistic affinity were synchronized with thousand years of Chinese history and civilization. Cultural and language wars were launched, too. The KMT wanted to make Taiwan more Chinese than China, ravaged as China was by the Cultural Revolution and ruled by classless people. Taiwan was the free China, the China where Chinese traditions were practiced and revered and where the Chinese language exhibited civilization and distinction.

Much has changed since the 1980s. Economic strength brought demands for greater civic freedom. Political symbols were reinterpreted to accommodate pluralism. The KMT, which initiated policy changes and political reforms either voluntarily or under pressure from public opinion, saw what resistance to changes and reforms were doing to the party and its fortunes, a rendezvous perhaps with the consequences of its long dealings with the CCP. Opposition political parties were legitimized, among the most influential the Democratic Progressive Party (DPP), which adhered to a platform of independence and advocated a quintessential Taiwanese identity that would abolish the influence of Chinese. The DPP emerged as a serious player in the 1980s, contended for domination in the 1990s, and became the ruling party in the year 2000. All aspects of cultural, national and language policies and practices became the objects of renewed contention. This time, the government was forced to reinvent Taiwan according to a democratized, multicultural blueprint. To paraphrase Heidegger, Taiwan today never is; it is always in a state of becoming.

Things were no less orderly at the professional, academic level. Waves of theories came, were challenged and were discarded. Structuralism was out, replaced by post-structuralism, post-modernism, and multiculturalism. This prompted a resurgence of energy on rethinking the well-defined, well-bounded model on language and identity in a democratized and pluralistic context. In linguistics the case of Chinese proved a counterexample to many theories based on European case studies. The ambiguous state of dialect and language seen from the Taiwanese perspective was a conventional linguistic replica after the Indo-European model which conflates a political center with linguistic factors such as mutual intelligibility, shared orthography and common roots.[2] This became problematic when advocates for previously marginalized varieties such as Hakka and Tai-yu[3] began demanding rights and representation in education and pubic settings, supporting their cases with evidence of a distinct history of writing as the basis of a language system rather than a subgroup of Chinese.[4] Mutual unintelligibility among speakers of northern and southern varieties is further cited from speakers who are conscious not only of their linguistic difference but also of the class distinctions emanating from Taiwan economic success since the 1980s. Contention for power in a democratized context further brings challenges to a default China-center/Mandarin-only language policy long held by the KMT administration, with radical dissent deeming the former as "foreign" and unfit for the island's people. On the one hand, this rhetoric bears much nationalistic fever with contention for a political center still undecided; on the other, it resembles the recurring tension between a centralized northern political center and the liberal, westernized cultural centers in the south.[5] With all their differences in check and economic interests at stake, Chinese on both sides of the Strait became more like economic partners than family members. Today, new metaphors are needed to help us get a better understanding of reality.

This book is thus a personal and professional account, for better, worse or ugly, of the ambivalence of belonging to a time of uncertainty. In addition, it tries to depict how language and national policies influence our ways of being and speaking. In turn, it shows how our choices of language and identity have changed the course of policies at the highest level.

Chapters of the book would not have been possible without the encouragement and guidance of teachers, friends and colleagues at various institutes. Professor Charles Bird in linguistics and Bonnie Kendal in anthropology at Indiana University took the time and effort to help me see the limitations of theory and realize the force of language in socio-political contexts. Lectures on modern Chinese history by Professor Jeffrey Wasserstrom at IU came as a lighting rod that broadened my perspectives on the tumults of Chinese history. Professor Samuel Obeng's works on political discourse in Ghana serve as continuing inspiration. Matthew Goodrum and John Hamilton have been most helpful with editing advice. Neil Kubler at Williams has never failed to answer any question on Chinese. His seminal work on languages in contact, with emphasis on Mandarin in Taiwan, continues to be an important point of reference for studying language variety in Chinese. Elise Breen has been more than a staunch friend through thick and thin, and a firm believer in what will work even at times when things just seem to work to the contrary.

I want to thank the Institute of International Asian Studies (IIAS) in Leiden and the National Science Council (NSC) in Taipei for a generous study grant in 2004 with which the book proposal was first conceived. The six month stay at Leiden was an eye-opening experience. The director, Wim Stokoff, and the staff were more than hospitable and professional. David Hymans, David Su, Lena Scheen, Walter Feldberg, Xiaozhen Ma, and Rima Soset all made things enjoyable. I learned that great scholarship can be found outside of a library—quality time at a café over good coffee or wine can produce long lasting, ingenious work. Michael Chang has been most helpful and generous in such settings, discussing aspects of Taiwanese consciousness. Dylan Tsai's insistence on the importance of cultivating genuine scholarship over a good meal proved to be an effective way of forging allies from among various theoretical camps. Henning Kloter's work on written Taiwanese alerted me to the complexity and history of

Chinese dialect writings. Mark Sebba at Lancaster University and Xiaoling Zhang at Nottingham University were generous to invite me to share findings of various chapters at their respective institutes.

Lastly, this book wouldn't have been possible without the help and encouragement of friends and colleagues at Soochow University. Don Gilleland, Stephen Schaufele, and Professor Yuan He-hsiang and Professor John Deeney have been generous with their time to clarify concepts and points of language. Karen Chan was most efficient with formatting and correspondences. Professor Liu Ching-cheng has been a constant source for things Chinese. Dr. Frank Muyard at the French Center for Contemporary China Studies (CEFC) was generous with critical questions and with his insights on the differences and similarities between Quebec and Taiwan. Dr. Alain Takam, Professor Bjorn Jernudd and Professor Murray Rubinstein were more than helpful with many suggestions on previous drafts. Two reviews from Lexington Books made the revision better-rounded. A grant from CCKF (Chiang Ching-Kuo International Scholarly Foundation) is acknowledged. I am also grateful to the editors and staff at Lexington Books (Patrick, Julie, Jessica and Ariel) for making the publication process as efficient and smooth as possible.

Notes

1. A friend from Beijing University, upon visiting Taipei, shared with me a *shunkouliu* (common expression), which captured the essence of the difference among major cities across the Strait these days. *Dao Beijing caizhidao guanxiao, dao Shanghai caizhidao qianshao, dao Taipei caizhidao wenge haizaigao.* (One realizes how trivial one's title is in Beijing, how little one's fortune is in Shanghai, and that a Cultural Revolution is still going on in Taipei.)

2. More discussion on the complexity of language and dialect in Chinese will be covered in Chapter 1.

3. I am using "Tai-yu" in this book to refer to Hoklo, a language used by people from Fujian Province, who constitute the largest ethnic group in Taiwan. There is a more often used but confusing term "Taiwanese" that literally means "languages spoken in Taiwan" but often refers to just the Hoklo variety. As most Taiwan natives are fluent in more than one language and are accustomed to inter-ethnic marriage, the use of "Taiwanese" in its monolingual and essentializing ethnolinguistic sense doesn't really represent linguistic reality, nor does the monolithic label reflect the ethnic tensions involved. Other sources of contention are that "Taiwanese" is set in opposition to Mandarin to challenge its authority and contain its domination while speakers of Hakka mostly, and of aboriginal languages to a lesser extent, feel marginalized by the label "Taiwanese."

4. More discussion on the implications of this issue will come in Chapter 5.

5. According to Li (2004, p. 99), "Prior to the Chinese Middle Ages the pronunciation of Changan (present-day Xian), capital of successive Chinese dynasties, competed with the accent of cultural Luoyang for linguistic supremacy. In the end it was the language of the cultural capital that won out. History repeated itself in the late Ming dynasty, when the capital was moved from cultural hub Nanjing to the new political center Beijing—the

culturally-dominant Nanjing accent held out for some 400 years before finally losing ground to the language of the capital, resulting in Nanjing-Beijing hybrid that is the basis of present-day Modern Standard Chinese" (Coblin, 2000 p. 542).

Introduction

This book examines the relationship between language choice and identity politics in Taiwan as the island democratizes and contemplates its vulnerable status quo within a tangled web of contending histories, facing an uncertain future. Definitions and boundaries of nation/state, dialect/language, and ethnicity are facing challenges as interest groups compete over material and symbolic resources. Well-bounded and defined linguistic or ethnic categories and the notion of one language/one nation/one people have serious consequences for speakers of Chinese as they face conflicting claims of authority and legitimacy attached to seemingly mundane linguistic transactions.

The book argues that language choice is inherently political because of its function as symbolic capital for the exercise of or resistance to power and its position with other forms of language practices in a linguistic market. A choice of language—from phonological shibboleth, Mandarin and/or Tai-yu, to choice of official language—cuts to the heart of contested cultural notions of self and other, with profound implications for nationalism, national unity and ethnolinguistic purism. The book further argues that because of the Chinese diaspora and Taiwan's connections to China, Japan and the United States, arguments and sentiments over language choice and identity have consequences for Taiwan's international and transnational status. They are symbolic acts of imagining Taiwan's past as she looks forward to the future.

The book is addressed to undergraduate and graduate students of sociolinguistics and specialists in the ethnography of communication and rhetoric; it will also be of broad interest to anthropologists, political scientists and East Asianists. The book brings new perspectives to—and invites comparative study within—the general study of language choice through its empirical focus on Chinese socio-political contexts and cultural practices. To the study of language planning and policy, the book offers concrete analysis of how individuals facing language choices come to terms with changing values and definitions of identity; it thus differs from leading works on East Asia that have addressed language policy on the road to modernization, focusing their efforts on either the status or corpus of blueprints for language varieties. Within East Asian and international political studies, this book should bring new perspectives on how creative language choices can make or break national, international and transnational relations, and should generate further discussion on collective identities in rapidly changing Greater China communities.

Chapter Overview

1. To *-er* is to err: acts of identity in Chinese
2. Language choice in Mandarin and Tai-yu
3. Language choices of Chen Shui-bian
4. Language choices and politics
5. From nationalism to multiculturalism: making choices in language policy
6. A hybrid Chinese for the twenty-first century

Chapter 1 introduces contested views of what comprises the Chinese language—what is mere dialect, and what constitutes Chinese identity—through the prism of the linguistic choice "to *-er* or not to *-er.*" For speakers of Standard Mandarin, the use of the word final *-er*, a characteristic of speakers from Beijing, is comparable to speakers of French emphasizing the "uvlar" /r/ to imitate Parisian French, or the dropping of the postvocalic /r/ among speakers of English. This chapter deconstructs this seemingly innocent phonological variation, and argues for translinguistic and post structural models to analyze the meaning of changing linguistic and cultural entities within contested social contexts. In particular, I adopt Bourdieu's approach of reflexive analysis, which argues that people endow situations with potency, altering their perceptions of situations and their reactions to them (1992: p. 136), and Bakhtin's notions of translinguistics and heteroglossia, useful concepts to study speakers' adjustments to uncertainty in fluid speech communities. The framework allows us to see verbal behavior as relations of force between speakers and their respective groups actualized in transfigured form (*ibid*: p. 142).

Chapter 2 surveys the literature on codeswitching in Taiwan and its well-researched socio-pragmatic aspects, as well as its less-known but increasingly important socio-political dimensions. Codeswitching as a communication strategy mixes official and non-official languages in different types of discourse to express solidarity, ethnic identity, professionalism or humor, while codeswitching as an interpersonal strategy can help draw, negotiate and overcome boundaries for socio/pragmatic/political purposes. The chapter begins with a sketch of language use and choice in Taiwan's multilingual society, followed by a theoretical orientation on key works on codeswitching and a survey of previous studies on codeswitching between Mandarin and Taiwanese. This chapter highlights their major findings, especially on the functions and motivations of codeswitching in domains such as political campaigning, and how the study of codeswitching can contribute to our understanding of ethnic identity, language policy and change.

Chapter 3 focuses on codeswitching by Taiwanese presidential candidates to illustrate how language choice relates to ethnic identity, national security and the struggle for power. Specifically, I contrast the use of Mandarin and Tai-yu by President Chen Shui-bian of the Democratic Progressive Party (DPP) in 2001 campaigning speeches. I conclude that Chen's constant use of Taiwanese—and to a lesser extent other varieties of Chinese—in public and political discourse has elevated Tai-yu from the "dialect" status accorded to it by KMT language policy to "a language of the people," and has led to the resurgence of ethnic consciousness. His deft choice of language combined with analogy, slang and metaphor can help to break or overcome boundaries, evade responsibility, and heighten tensions among contending parties. By focusing on politicians' language choices, we see that codeswitching serves pragmatic/strategic functions such as raising ethnic consciousness to mobilize supporters and the creation of political personas.

Chapter 4 further analyzes language choice among politicians. Following M. Heller, who has done extensive work on the power struggle between English and French speaking populations in Canada, I propose to study codeswitching in political contexts as part of power struggles where ethnic groups fight over material and symbolic resources, and legitimacy (Heller 1988; 1992). Moreover, I argue that political discourse is an ideal forum to observe the socio-political implications of codeswitching since political professionals tend to polarize issues, heighten emotions and exploit fears to solicit votes. The power struggle analysis will shed light on how individuals, given the constraints and predicaments of given language practices, strive to reject, negotiate or accept language choices. In addition, I employ Bakhtin's notion of "voice" and "dialogue" to help analyze how conflicting ideologies over Chinese/Taiwanese—the former premised on cultural-historical determinacy, the latter on political pragmatism—enter speakers' political oratory. Chapter 4 thus treats codeswitching as part of political struggles over legitimacy and resources, situating individual language use and choice in broader socio-political context to enhance our understanding of the relationship between ideologies of language and ideologies of the nation-state.

Chapter 5 analyzes language choices in a multicultural context by using Taiwan's democratizing experiences and its redefinition and reinterpretation of history and political symbols. We look into the socio-political underpinnings of policy making on language choice and identity politics. We treat discourse on language as fraught with tensions between the state and various interest groups. That is, narratives for promoting or abolishing a certain form of language policy—assimilationism, pluralism, multiculturalism—become emotionally charged as they concern not only language per se, but how policy envisions and enacts ties of language to identity, morality and epistemology. Moreover, we point out that language policy in a multicultural context implies conflict and controversy as it becomes the object of contention not only over symbolic recognition of minorities but also over the appropriation of materials and status for official languages. The implications of this chapter are national as well as transnational, as we learn from debates on issues such as choices of official language, promotion of mother tongue education for minorities and implementation of bilingual education at various school levels. A language policy seen as such is not only a statement about a nation's past and future but also the state's responses to tensions between globalization and indigenization. Moreover, Taiwan's historical ties to China and contention among its ethnic groups are heightened as representations and resources face challenges. Our analyses shed light on the origins and transformation of Taiwanese national identity, the conceptualizing of linguistic variety in pivotal periods of the island's history, and the pressing issues of power, ethnicity, and class in an emerging democracy.

Based on the findings of the preceding chapters, the concluding chapter argues the need for multilingual speakers to relativize their perceptions of "genuine ethnic identity" via a "real language" and to broaden their inventory of social identities. The hegemonic myth of creating a standard language, an ideal speaker, and an invariant community rooted in the twentieth century obscures much of what is really happening in Chinese communities—whether in China, Hong Kong, or Taiwan. This essentialist mentality in defining nation and language is not only scientifically untenable; its political effects militate against recognition and respect for genuine ethnic and linguistic diversity. Finally, we argue that only by relocating to fairer grounds a set of polemic representations—in language choice, stereotypes and identities—and probing the socio-cultural forces acting upon or within an individual in making language choices can we begin to deconstruct myths and begin real dialogue.

Chapter 1
To –Er Is to Err: Acts of Identity in Chinese

The purpose of this chapter is to propose a new method for analyzing language choice and identity politics. The dialogic tension between individual agency and structural constraints is stressed. Rather than pointing out how rules should be followed, we adopt Bourdieu's theory of practice (1977) to argue that regularities of "usage" are not explained by rules, codes, or conventions but by embodied dispositions, which are not "followed" or "obeyed" but are actualized in speech (cf. Hanks, 2005, p. 72). By treating the suffixual -/r/ in standard Chinese as a socio-culturally constructed symbol rather than as an invariant and well-bounded linguistic code, this chapter probes into the many forces—economic, cultural and political—acting upon and within a multi-lingual speaker in performing acts of identity by way of a language choice in an emerging transnational Chinese context. Our objectives are achieved by laying out the fact that standard Chinese was established by authorities at Beijing and Taipei using the Beijing variety as oral and written bases for modernizing and unifying the nation. Although stability and unity were achieved, standard Chinese does leave speakers of southern varieties such as Cantonese and Southern Min at a linguistic disadvantage as mutual unintelligibility remains the greatest with their northern counterparts. People in Taiwan suffered more than just linguistic disadvantage. A high-handed implementation of standard Chinese after the KMT began its rule of the island after 1945 further lowered the status of speakers of Tai-yu, Hakka, and aboriginal languages. They became "minority" speakers who had to abolish not only their local languages but also their previous "national language"—Japanese as a result of a fifty years of colonization. Moreover, the KMT's defeat by the CCP in 1949, its loss of its U.N. seat to Beijing in 1972 and its loss of diplomatic ties with major nations such as the U.S., as well as its loss to the DPP in the 2000 and 2004 elections, all worked to make a well-defined nationalistic model on language and identity problematic.

Introduction

As linguists of Chinese have noted, the northern speech variety of Chinese often contains word final -erization, that is, adding a /r/ suffix to certain words, as in *fanguan-r* (restaurant) and *chaguan-r* (tea house). Chinese speakers don't really hear the word final /r/ sound spoken in many places outside of Beijing, any more than standard English language textbooks insist on a Boston /r/. For Chinese speakers, the use of word final /r/ is comparable to French speakers emphasizing the "uvular" /r/ to imitate Parisian French, or the dropping of the postvocalic /r/ in postvocalic positions among speakers of English in some of the east coast states of the U.S. However, this seemingly innocent phonological variation does more than just associate the speaker with a certain place, and can project not only relatively benign class difference but also strong emotions such as nationalism and moralism. We argue for a translinguistic and post-structural model to analyze the meaning of changing linguistic and cultural entities within contested social contexts. In particular, we adopt Bourdieu's approach of reflexive analysis, which argues that people endow situations with potency, altering their perceptions of situations and their reactions to them (Bourdieu and Wacquant, 1992, p. 136), and Bakhtin's notions of translinguistics and heteroglossia, useful concepts to study speakers' adjustments to uncertainty in fluid speech communities. The framework allows us to see verbal behavior as relations of force between speakers and their respective groups actualized in transfigured form (ibid, p. 142). Moreover, the translinguistic notion helps explain the "dialogic imagination" over a choice of a certain linguistic feature, and reveals much of the intertwined socio-historical contingencies in emerging transnational Chinese communities.

The Word-final -erization in Standard Mandarin Chinese

Dayle Barnes (1974, 1977) defines word-final -erization from a socio-structural perspective. Geographically, -erization can be heard in the speech of northern Chinese speakers in a number of Mandarin speaking areas of China, most notably among natives of Beijing, the national capital. However, -erization appears on the whole to be absent from many other Mandarin speaking areas, and completely absent from the sound system of the quite distinct Chinese "dialects" indigenous to several of the provinces of southeast China (1977, p. 211).

Chris Li (2004) traces this linguistic feature to its historical roots and identifies it as an Altaic element introduced to northern China by the invading Mongols and Manchus from the fourteenth century onward. It is not featured in traditional rhyme books or rhyme charts. Within the city of Beijing, the speech in Manchu and Mongol quarters exhibits considerably more *-er* than that of Han

Chinese quarters. This characterization of *-er* as a foreignism has given fuel to nationalistic sentiments and calls by archaists and xenophobes alike to purge the standard language of non-Chinese elements (ibid, p. 124). In present days, word-final -erization can be described as having the following properties: (1) it distinguishes northern (and hence government decreed "standard") speech from its southern counterparts; (2) it is used more often by the lower strata of society than by the educated classes; (3) it is not used consistently throughout northern China (and hence is difficult to standardize); and (4) it is a foreign element introduced relatively recently in China's long history to Chinese morphology (ibid, p. 125).

Qing Zhang (2005), while describing the linguistic practice of Chinese managerial professionals working for foreign businesses in Beijing, found that Beijingers identify two features with the smoothness[1] of so-called Chinese yuppie speech. The first is rhotacization of the syllable final (or -erization), and the second is lenition of retroflex obstruent initials. Rhotacization is not the only feature that contributes to the perception of "heavy r-sounding." Additionally, it involves lenition of a set of retroflex obstruents (2005, p. 441).

Through my own experience as a Chinese person born and raised in Taipei in the 1960s and as a linguist trained in the 1980s in the United States, I have come to notice some of the blind spots created by a normative approach in treating a linguistic feature such as word final -erization in Chinese. The issues lie in the contentions among language variations and their different associations in space and time. They place significant weight on a multilingual speaker's concerns over a language choice. Such a choice, to paraphrase Karl Marx, might not accord with one's own preference, as it often comes with a great deal of cultural and political baggage. The tumultuous history of modern China and the complexities associated with the Chinese diaspora—as well as issues of power and identity within emerging transnational Chinese communities such as Hong Kong, Beijing and Taipei—have implications and consequences even for the most seemingly objective linguistic choice, such as "to -er or not to -er."

I propose an interactional approach to the study of language variations rather than a structural or correlational functional approach. I suggest that it is best to probe into the translinguistic context of creating a standard language in Chinese in order to understand this linguistic phenomenon. Following Bakhtin (1981), Hill and Hill (1986) and Heath (1983), I argue for a dialogic model in order to deconstruct this issue from a viewpoint of "epistemological relativism." The meaning of suffixual -/r/—comparable as mentioned before to that of the postvocalic -/r/ in English in certain parts of the United States or the "received" uvular /r/ as opposed to the rolled /r/ in French—is local and contingent. I conclude that what a multilingual speaker faces in making a language choice is more characteristic of an ideological contest than of a well-defined linguistic exercise where, presumably, an absolute line can be demarcated within a static system of forms and meaning.

Chapter One

The Example

This perspective came home to me in a personal way when I was working on a project on Chinese language choices and adaptations in New York City. I had long been fascinated by how speakers of Chinese choose from an array of language options to act out their social identities, and a range of questions puzzled me. What's on their mind when they switch from one language to another?[2] How do they react to varieties of spoken or written Chinese, especially those different from the ones they are using? What kind of symbolic capital[3] do they risk in defining or defending one set of varieties but not the other? How would I go about getting to know these variations?

My mind was constantly occupied by these questions as I engaged in conversation an American student of Chinese at Columbia University. Our conversation warmed with our discovery of similar interests: Chinese languages, social discourse, language and power. I was intrigued by the way he talked, assuming that he was well educated, good mannered, and knowledgeable. I thought that he could be more than just a casual acquaintance; he could be a friend, a companion, an ally. After a short time, the conversation shifted to our plans for the summer. Then he said: "*Wo yao zai fanguan-r dagong*" (I will work in a restaurant). Hearing that -erized[4] word, which is characteristic of Beijing Mandarin, and which I associated negatively with the Beijing-based Communist Party, I immediately felt a gulf between us. Due to no fault of his own—he spoke the way he had been taught—our potential friendship stalled in perplexity and silence. There was no way, given my background, that I could be friends with a person whose speech characteristics constantly reminded me of an ideology I disliked.

To say I suspended this potential friendship because I did not or could not understand his Mandarin would be false. I understood it only too well. I was also keenly aware of the sensitivity of people who refrain from using -erization because they recognize this linguistic feature as an ideologically charged sign. Being born and educated in Taiwan, my impulse was to identify with those who, like me, spoke the kind of Mandarin devoid of the Beijing characteristic. This had everything to do with my anxiety about Taiwan's future and my grievances over China's past.[5] "To -er or not to -er" was not a question in my mind: to -*er* was to err.

My point is that the contested social meanings embedded in this linguistic sign /r/ have taken on specific social valuations and are perceived at a very conscious level (Labov 1972). It is more than an issue of correctness or a demonstration of linguistic competence. It is an act of identity (Le Page and Tabouret-Keller 1985). In other words, my cultural self[6] as a Taiwanese female and my language self as a Mandarin speaker from Taipei were in conflict with my linguistic self as a "competent and objective professional." It was more than a choice of a code, which still implies a set of laws which doom a speaker to obey; thus, his or her free will or language adaptations can only be surrendered under a set of prescribed patterns. I want to point out the duel of socio-political forces that act upon and within a speaker in his or her making of a linguistic choice. Mine was an ideological calculation of "how I should behave versus what I want to be." It was a consciousness, as Susan Gal proposes, of "how speakers respond symbolically to relations of domination between groups within the state, and how they understand their historic position and identity within a world structured around dependency and unequal development" (1988, p. 248).

My silence at that time with the American student in response to his Beijing Mandarin only reminded me of the many silences from other people, like myself, well-educated, sensitive, and sympathetic, yet labeled as the "other" Chinese. I chose silence in order to identify with the linguistic others. The making of such a choice cannot be understood apart from the socio-political evolution of the linguistic symbol -/r/ and its representations in various Chinese communities.

The Evolution of Standard Chinese

As mentioned, word final retroflexion, termed -erization by Barnes (1977), occurs in the northern variety of Chinese. It was adopted by the authorities in Beijing and Taiwan in the 1940s as the linguistic norm for Putonghua[7] and Guoyu, terms for Mandarin as the national language used by the the Chinese Communists and their Nationalist adversaries respectively. According to Li (2004), the split of China following the civil war lost by the Nationalists has meant that different linguistic norms continue to be used in mainland China and Taiwan: the 1926 standard in Taiwan, and the 1956 revision in China. The two standards, while both based on a Beijing pronunciation and superficially similar, do contain subtle differences. The norm in Taiwan is modeled on the language of the educated classes, which translates to a preference for the Nanjing-based literary stratum of Beijing Mandarin. The norm on the mainland, due to anti-bourgeois sentiments following the Communist takeover, favors the language of the lower socio-economic classes, and subsequent revisions of standard pronunciation in 1957, 1962 and 1985 (2004, p. 103). Further linguistic differences between the development of Mandarin in Taipei and Beijing also include the adoption of local and foreign influences (Kubler, 1981, 1985).

As mentioned in the beginning, -erization is usually absent from the speech of many other Mandarin-speaking areas (such as Singapore) and is completely absent from the distinct linguistic varieties of Chinese indigenous to language areas of southeast China such as Guangdong and Hong Kong, and to Taiwan where the Yue and Min varieties of Chinese are practiced. The selection of a linguistic norm as a national language (Guoyu), as is the case in Taiwan, or as a common language (Putonghua), as is the case in China, is not a straightforward linguistic exercise. The choice of a standard variety against which other varieties are measured and valued is a prescribed linguistic phenomenon. Its codification and imposition have to do with the socio-political status of a linguistic variety at a certain time and place.

Also as previously mentioned, the linguistic discrepancy for Chinese speakers is greater between speakers of southern varieties and their northern counterpart, thus making it more difficult for southerners to learn a language distant from their everyday usage. At the beginning of the twentieth century, this was cited as one of the major objections to replacing *wenyan* with *baihua*, with the former seen by reformers as the privileged literary language distant from local colloquialisms but protected in high social status by an examination system[8] requiring the utmost learning to master it. The latter, in comparison, was conceived and designed to rid China from all the vices associated with *wenyan*, aiming to be closer to everyday speech and thus easier for common folks to learn in the effort to free the country from its feudalistic past. According to Chen (1999), the argument was that since *wenyan* was dissociated from all of the contemporary dialects, the dialectal background of learners would not make any difference in its acquisition; with *baihua*, on the other hand, southerners would be at a linguistic disadvantage in comparison with native speakers of Northern Mandarin. This concern, as it turned out, was overridden by the urgent need for a written language that was closer to the vernacular of the majority of the population and thus more suitable for a modernizing society (p. 141).

In addition, Lehmann (1975) points out that the written language has been seen as a unifying factor throughout Chinese history, making the issue of reforming written Chinese doubly important.[9] In the spread of a common spoken language, the dialect of Peking (Beijing) has had a natural preeminence dating at least from the location of the capital in Peking in the fourteenth century. Side by side with the literary language the spoken vernacular was followed in certain kinds of literature. In the early days of the Republic a campaign spearheaded by the May Fourth Movement in 1919 advocated the use of the modern spoken language as the sole basis for written Chinese (p. 42).

Linguistically, the Yue variety (Cantonese) and Min variety (Tai-yu)[10] of Chinese preserve more distinct linguistic traces of ancient Chinese than those of the northern varieties such as Beijing Mandarin. For example, Cantonese and Tai-yu have more elaborate tonal repertoires than their Beijing counterpart. Both preserve many word final consonants from Old Chinese which are absent in the Beijing variety. In the case of Cantonese, the direct object is followed by indirect object as in the sentence, *neih bei min ngoh*[11] (you give face [to] me), further distinguishing it from Standard Mandarin which retains the indirect object followed by direct object as in *ni gei wo mianzi* (you give me face).

According to Robert Cheng, Tai-yu differs from Mandarin in the following aspects: contrast between habitual and future action, contrast between present and past tense, use of preverbal auxiliary verbs, and the obligatory use of auxiliary verbs as operators (Cheng 1985, pp. 353-68). In addition to the grammatical differences, dental retroflexations and suffixual -erization are also absent from Tai-yu (Kubler 1981).

Yue and Min have been widely used not only by Chinese in the southeast provinces of the mainland, such as Guangzhou and Fujian, but are also associated with the Chinese diaspora dating from the end of the eighteenth century. In North America, Australia, and Southeast Asia, one can hear these two varieties along with other varieties of Chinese practiced daily. Cantonese has been the native language for the Chinese in Hong Kong, though it has never had an official status such as that held by British English during the colonization or that was granted to Putonghua after 1997[12] (when Hong Kong returned to the People's Republic of China).

A similar sociolinguistic situation occurred historically in Taiwan. As discussed by Kubler, on two occasions in Taiwan's recent history, non-native languages were widely promoted by different governments originally located outside the island (1985, p. 156). First, Japanese was declared the official language during Japan's colonization (1895-1945) of Taiwan. Then, Standard Mandarin replaced Japanese in official and national linguistic status after World War II. DeFrancis (1984) provides similar observations. The native speakers of Mandarin who took over Taiwan after 1945 comprised one or two million persons compared with the five or six million inhabitants already there. Most of the latter were native speakers of what is variously called Tai-yu, Fujianese or Southern Min and is spoken in the adjacent mainland province of Fujian, from which the ancestors of many Han Chinese living in Taiwan today started to migrate some three centuries ago. In 1945, under the Nationalists, Guoyu was imposed on this non-Mandarin majority as the exclusive language of education (DeFrancis 1984, p. 59).

On the Chinese mainland, standardization of Chinese, based on the northern speech of Beijing, was promoted with the circulation of the official language policy of 1956. By adopting the term Putonghua, the Chinese Communist leaders meant to play down the inherent exclusiveness of a standard language and elevate the most "viable and potent" elements from the working class and peasants (Ramsey 1987, p. 15). In fact, the Committee on Language Reform, placed directly under the State Council, was founded in 1954. Its task was to make the Chinese language serve the workers and peasants and to further socialist construction (Lehman 1975, p. 52).

A Case in Chinese

It is notable that authorities in Beijing, Hong Kong, and Taipei hold opposing opinions as to what is authentic Chinese and what is merely a dialect. The definition of which variety of Chinese qualifies as the national language, and which is, by default, an abbreviation, a dialect, or "non-standard" is not a straightforward linguistic exercise. Standard Mandarin, alias Guoyu in Taiwan and Putonghua in China, is a prescribed language and is based on a Beijing variety. In the general linguistic paradigm, the contested issue of language or dialect is not interesting. As Milroy and Milroy point out: "One consequence of the doctrine of arbitrariness is the linguist's working assumption that no language or dialect can be shown to be better or worse than another on linguistic grounds alone" (Milroy and Milroy 1985, p. 19). In reality, it is very difficult to test this scientific assumption empirically since the antithesis to the assumption, that one linguistic variety is superior to the other, is like two sides of a coin. Generally, in a linguist's mind, the *value* as opposed to the *signification* of a linguistic variety is purely ideological, and not scientifically important.

Thus, all things being equal, varieties of Chinese—just like those of English, Latin and its derivatives, or Arabic—are entitled to qualify as standard languages, regardless of the evolution of economics, politics or history. If treating one language as superior to the other is ideological but not scientific, then the notion of Standard English, Standard Latin, Standard Arabic, or Standard Chinese is certainly ideological too. As Milroy and Milroy write:

> The spread of English is due, not to its superiority as a language system, but to the greater economic and political success of its speakers in recent centuries. In a similar way, Classical Latin became the official language of a great empire; yet, its great prestige did not ensure its ultimate survival in the face of political and economic change. (Milroy and Milroy 1985, p. 19)

Norman (1988) compared this linguistic ambiguity of language and dialect in Chinese to that of the Romance languages: "both have their roots in a large-scale imperial expansion . . . in both instances the imperial language was carried by armies and settlers to areas previously occupied by speakers of different languages; . . . in both cases, the newly developing vernaculars existed alongside an antiquated written language and were profoundly influenced by it. In view of these parallels, it would not be surprising if we found about the same degree of diversity among the Chinese dialects as we do among the Romance languages, and in fact I believe this to be the case" (Norman 1988, p. 187).

Li (2004) points out that political unity, genetic affiliation and shared orthography decide whether two speech varieties are to be labeled dialects of the same language or not. Thus under the Chinese system "Chinese" is a single "language," with Mandarin, Wu, Min, Yue, Xiang, Gan, and Hakka being dialects of that language, a classification differing markedly from the western approach to the issue, which treats "Chinese" as a language family, and Mandarin, Wu, Min, Yue, Xiang, Gan, and Hakka as separate languages, considering that they are not mutually intelligible despite shared orthography and common roots (2004, p. 111).

To call Cantonese and Min major Chinese dialects is like calling French, Italian and Spanish major Latin dialects or, worse yet, major French dialects, major Italian dialects, or major Spanish dialects (depending on which end of the spectrum one is viewing). The socio-cultural evolution of varieties of Chinese parallels that of the varieties of Latin. A change of name from major languages to major dialects lowers the "dialectal" varieties in the linguistic hierarchy, implying as well the subordination of their speakers to the speakers of "the language" on a socio-psychological ladder. This kind of labeling goes on every day in Taipei and has profound consequences for the ways people view themselves and others. It colors their interactions in particular ways. Their daily linguistic transactions fluctuate as the socio-economic forces change, with the fluctuations contingent on the ever-changing socio-cultural predicament. If Rome were still the political center of European power, speakers of the Italianate varieties of the Romance language might be doing just what the speakers of Chinese are doing in a multilingual community such as Taipei. Speakers of Guoyu looked down their noses at Tai-yu speakers; conversely, reverse language discrimination also came to the scene with the quibble of dominance. Moreover, a standard language based on the northern Beijing variety put southern speakers at a linguistic disadvantage simply because it is more difficult for them to learn a script or a national language that is not close to their everyday speech. In fact, this might just be as problematic when the reverse situation occurs, as Lehmann (1975) documented from this historical example of efforts to popularize Putonghua:

> The county of Datian in Fujian province was cited as an example of the progress achieved. It has three major and over ten minor dialects—"people separated by a blade of grass could not understand each other." A cadre from the north needed three to seven interpreters to make a speech. Party leaders took an active role in promoting Putonghua, concentrating on schools, evening schools, and public gathering places; and . . . in the movement to criticize Lin Piao and Confucius there was further advance in the popularization of Putonghua. In a recent radio report a county official addressed 120,000 people without need of an interpreter (p. 49).

Authenticity and antiquity aside, speakers of southern varieties also experienced, in the way of written representation, church Romanization in the nineteenth century with missionaries coming to the island and the costal areas on the mainland, among other colonial influences.[13] At best, these representations tended at least until very recently to be treated with the usual condescension by literates who saw anything other than the Chinese character as unworthy of a great civilization, or by authorities who took the position that they simply didn't exist. To provide examples: When Tai-oan-hu-sia Kau-hoe-po, the first Taiwanese newspaper in Romanization, was published in 1885, the editor and publisher, the Rev. Thomas Barclay, exhorted readers of the newspaper not to "look down at Peh-oe-ji; do not regard it as a childish writing" (cf. Chiung 2001, p. 508). In the volume on literature in *zhongguo da baikequanshu* (Encyclopedia Sinica) (Y. Zhou), which represents the most up-to-date and comprehensive scholarship on the study of literature in China, non-Mandarin literature does not even receive a passing mention (Chen 1999, p. 115). At its worst, non-Chinese writing had been treated as threat to Chinese culture and Chinese nationalism. The New Testament ("Sin-Iok") was once seized, in 1975, because Peh-oe-ji was regarded as a challenge to the orthodox status of Han characters (Chiung 2001, p. 509). Dialect or language in the Chinese case is more than a linguistic question and can't be accounted for by the linguistic criteria used for European languages.

Conflicting Meanings of Suffixual -Erization in Standard Chinese

As mentioned in a previous footnote, this chapter follows Barnes (1977) in focusing only on nouns -erized in word final position. This linguistic phenomenon is characteristic in northern Chinese speech and notably in Beijing, the capital of the People's Republic of China. Not all word final nouns are subject to word-final -erization in northern speech. Chao provides extended examples for lexical distributions of -erization (1976, pp. 216-49). According to some of my informants from Beijing, speakers of both Beijing patois and Beijing language demonstrate -erization. For example, when I said *dashiguan-r* (embassy), I was laughed at by a Beijing speaker who later told me that dashiguan, as opposed to fanguan-r (restaurant) or chaguan-r (tea house), is a grand place and people (speakers of Beijing language as opposed to Beijing patois) do not -erize this word. When I said *shifu-r* (master), a term which has gained currency among people in China, she commented on the improper usage of such a fashion as "the uneducated trying to imitate the speech of the learned." I later asked this speaker what came to her mind when she heard this "mistake" from other people (those who -erize in the "wrong" manner, and therefore, by her definition, speak the patois of Beijing). "You are either not from Beijing or you are from a low class in Beijing." "To -er or not to -er" is neither a dilemma nor a mistake in her mind. According to her, only those who do not speak the Beijing language have to worry about this issue. Thus, word-final -erization for a Beijing speaker is a linguistic marker not only to differentiate who speaks the Beijing language but also to differentiate different classes. (You are either not from Beijing or you are a speaker of Beijing patois.)

As mentioned above, suffixual -erization was absent in the Min dialect and has been a highly marked linguistic feature, even among those who were born in the sixties and learned to speak Guoyu at school. Guoyu was first imposed in Taiwan after 1945 to replace Japanese as the "national" language, when Taiwan was freed from Japanese colonization. As a result of the colonization (1895-1945), most adults living in Taiwan then had learned Japanese in school prior to their now learning Guoyu, the language promoted by the new government in Taiwan. The distinction between the "Taiwanese," those who lived in Taiwan prior to 1945, and the bulk of the Chinese mainlanders who came to Taiwan after 1945, soon became a very sensitive socio-political issue.[14] The February Twenty-eighth (2/28) Incident in 1947, when the Nationalist Party used force to repress discontented Taiwanese, highlighted ethnic tensions among the Chinese in Taiwan. As a result, Guoyu, spoken with word-final -erization and a set of dental retroflexations, was regarded as highly marked, not only linguistically but also socio-culturally. One of my informants from Taiwan commented: "When I was young, if I heard people speak with -erization, I knew that person was a Mainlander. None of my friends would speak in such a fashion."

Demonstration of "correct" pronunciation of Chinese is often compounded with pride and prejudice regarding one's native place. e.g., *Ni(n) shi nali ren?* in Taiwanese Mandarin as opposed to *Ni(n) shi na-r ren?* in Standard Mandarin. Suffixual -erization in this context receives a social referent in differentiating the Mainlanders in general who came to Taiwan after 1945 and the Taiwanese who came to Taiwan before then.[15] Over the years, interethnic marriage and the rise of new generations of Taiwanese born and raised in Taiwan after the late 1940s emigration from the Chinese mainland have made the distinction between Mainlander and Taiwanese less socio-culturally sensitive. The increased wealth enjoyed by the Chinese in Taiwan since the 1980s and their search for a legitimate identity on the international stage have consolidated and revised the status of "Mandarin in Taiwan" and have added a new referent to Guoyu. -Erization in this context associates this sound with a group of political authorities in Beijing who are distrusted and resented for their social and political acts especially since the 1960s.

What does suffixual -erization mean to an American student of Chinese? Is it a put-on speech act which native speakers of Chinese love to perform in order to gain an upper-hand over their non-Chinese counterparts, a *deja-vu* sound (the post-vocalic /r/ in English or the uvular /r/ in Parisian French?) whose social referents and meanings are as intriguing as its Chinese counterpart? Or is it a peculiar linguistic marker identified with a particular place, Beijing, which has great symbolic power in modern Chinese civilization and shows a northern Chinese bias in Chinese political history, reinforced by the actions of the Chinese Communist Party?[16]

When I first studied Chinese in school in Taiwan in the 1970s, I always detested this /r/ sound. It reminded me of the way my mother spoke English. She and my dad were both from a small city in the Rhode Island-Massachusetts area. She tended to add an /r/ to words ending with an open vowel like the word "idea" (/aidir/), and dropped the /r/ when the word ended with an /r/ sound as in "car" (/kaa/). I always felt embarrassed to hear her speak like that. One of my Chinese teachers from Beijing didn't personally use the -erization style of speaking with other people. She only wanted us, the foreign students of Chinese, to learn it.[17] I felt it sounded so unnatural. Plus, nobody spoke in this fashion on the street. However, I could accept teachers who -erized their Chinese all the time, not just in front of the foreign students. Once when I was walking in Hong Kong, I heard a person behind me -erizing almost every word. I turned around and found out that it was a foreigner speaking Chinese. He spoke like someone from Beijing. Someone told me later that this person's speech sounded like Beijing patois. But my attitude has changed over the years as I met more speakers from Beijing and become friends with them. I remember the first time I was actually attracted by the sound, which I think is acceptable to me now. It was when I heard the six-year old son of one of my friends from Beijing talking. -Erized words just came out his mouth naturally. I said to myself, "This is the very thing that we are knocking ourselves out for as language students, and this little boy just produces it without any difficulty or confusion."

In sum, in this section, we have provided socio-political contingencies for a variety of meanings associated with the suffixual erization. In the next section, we will look into relevant theoretical concepts in order to provide further insights on the use of a charged linguistic sign.

The Translinguistic Approach

In recent years, there has been rising interest in the work of the Russian literary scholar and linguist, M. M. Bakhtin, and his translinguistic approach to the study of language (Bakhtin 1981). The voice of literary prose is a central structural element in his theory, which is not a set of terms for the description of language but is instead a study of language in domains beyond the bounds of form and content (Hill 1987, p. 92). Such a notion, therefore, is different from the notion of meta-messages (Bateson 1972), which still implies a grammatical structure determining the shape of messages.

Central to a translinguistic approach is the identification and description of voice or, better yet, voices. The translinguistic approach regards speakers as in control of a range of ways of speaking and writing and, consequently, seeks an account of the possibilities open to them to juxtapose complementary and conflicting voices (Hill and Hill 1986). The notions of heteroglossia and polyphony are designed to capture the multiplicity of possibilities that reside within communities and within individuals.

Polyphonic discourse is characteristic of all speech communities, including academic ones. Within the discipline of linguistics, structuralists organize their metaphors so as to talk about language as a system of rules which describe ideal and invariant objects. Functionalists organize their metaphors to predict variation in language as determined by well-defined and unchanging variables (such as gender and class) in a society where everyone defines gender and class the same way. Modes of linguistic discourse treating languages one way or another may also be seen as on-going dialogues where different voices come into play in shaping a contested paradigm. Several of Bakhtin's terms and metaphors, such as dialogue, discourse, and dialogic relation, are useful in understanding the dynamics of a charged language choice.

Dialogue, apart from its normal meaning of an exchange of utterances, does not necessarily involve the speaker and the listener in any oral physical sense; rather, it can also refer to inner speech communication (Vygotsky 1986). For example, when I choose "to -er or not to -er," I engage my mind in a dialogue with what I internalized as "Chinese speaking" learned in years of Taiwan schooling. In other words, I engage in a conversation or dialogue with family, friends and teachers from whom I constructed a cultural identity as a middle-class Taiwanese female, though none of them may be physically present. It was *this* dialogue that guided my language choice during the previously-cited conversation I had with the American student of Chinese, even though the latter was physically present. My prior social experiences organize my linguistic transactions with others according to internal voices and different social consciousnesses.

In other words, although I understood my actual interlocutor and his Putonghua, I comprehended the form and content of what it represented at a given moment in comparison with previous dialogues. The prior dialogues I remembered from school days in Taiwan and the dialogue I had learned to expect from well educated, knowledgeable students of Chinese guided my perception of the situation at hand and constituted my expectations for future interaction. Each such dialogue then leads to a more complex one and is further internalized and constantly recalled and reinterpreted to enrich the dynamics of a relationship. The dialogues thicken understandings and complicate strategies for interaction.

Discourse in a Bakhtian sense means a specific point of view constituted by a particular social consciousness (Voloshinov 1986). For example, my graduate training in various formal linguistic discourses equipped me with theoretical insights as to what a language is and what dialects are. My Taiwanese middle-class upbringing imparted a strong sense of what it means to be a genuine Chinese. Enduring relationships with family, friends, and teachers in a community outside mainland China further inculcated in me aesthetic and emotional ties to various Chinese usages. These intellectual and emotional investments conditioned my language behavior, and I further internalized them as a persuasive frame of reference to interpret those who behaved differently from me, either linguistically or culturally. This set of implicit socio-cultural ideologies underlies my social identity and guides my language choices. The notion of dialogic relation is prominent in a heteroglossic situation. That is, the meaning of word-final /r/ in Standard Mandarin is not as static or well-defined as an objective linguist would assume. Historical contexts give -/r/ life and substance. As Voloshinov points out: "In actual fact, . . . contexts of usage for one and the same word often contrast with one another. . . . Contexts do not stand side by side in a row, as if unaware of one another, but are in a state of constant tension, or incessant interaction and conflict" (Voloshinov 1986, p. 80).

The purely objective linguist throws the issue of historical context overboard along with the notion of parole, the non-standard, non-systematic speech. What is left in this analysis is a monologizing discourse where each repetition of the same word aims at the same direction. This, of course, is far from the truth. The polemic nature of a symbol profiles the dialogic relations to the interested institutions and/or individuals. Standard Mandarin typified by suffixual -erization has gained several referents over the years. The dramatic historical events that have taken place since 1945 shaped and are still shaping the meaning of suffixual -erization in Standard Mandarin. It can signify authority, prestige, prejudice, bureaucracy, or hypocrisy in instances such as the designation of Standard Mandarin as the national language by the Chinese government in Taiwan, the elevation in social status of the working class and the peasants during China's communization, and the designation of Putonghua as the common language for all the people in China by the Chinese Communist Party. -Erization further signifies attitudes formed when elements of the Communist Party instigated and directed radicals during the Cultural Revolution (1966-1976) to denounce old values and abolish the use of native place as a reference or source for social identity; when the US and the PRC normalized diplomatic ties in 1979[18] and when the demonstration in Tiananmen Square was suppressed on June 4, 1989. These attitudes toward -erization took on further nuances with the return of Hong Kong to Beijing in 1997; with the status of Cantonese, the language used by most Hong Kong locals, still left ambiguous; and with Beijing and Taipei trying a more conciliatory and pragmatic approach toward economic growth on both sides of the Strait, yet at the same time remaining hostile politically over issues of legitimacy and representation. Only by relocating -/r/ in a given socio-cultural discourse can we begin to understand its multivocality.

Summary and Conclusions

By situating the suffixual -erization in Standard Mandarin in different times and spaces, we find several social referents for this linguistic phenomenon. A speaker from Beijing, for whom suffixual -erization is an unmarked feature, can use it to distinguish different classes (e.g., working class from the educated) or native place (from Beijing or not). A speaker from Taipei, for whom -erization is a highly marked feature, can use it to distinguish those who came from Taiwan before 1945 (the Taiwanese) from those who came after 1945 (the Mainlanders) or can use it to distinguish we (the Chinese in Taiwan) from they (the Chinese bureaucrats in Beijing). For an American speaker of Chinese, who has to relativize sets of communicative rules against his/her social class background and intentions, what really marks the distinction in "to -er or not to -er" is not the formal difference in phonetics but the dynamic socio-political dimension which speaks through it.

By deconstructing the ambiguities in standard Chinese and presenting their indeterminacy in practical implications, this chapter provides an alternative analysis to the study of language choice and acts of identity. It aims to show that in the case of speaking Guoyu or Putonghua "to -er or not to -er" is analogous to "to be or not to be;" that is, how you -er is how you mark your class or social status. Recognizing the inequality in access to and command of a standard language, this chapter advocates locating the study of language choice beyond bounded forms and meanings, and instead situates it in a context of economic and political power relations. Guoyu is undergoing constant deconstruction and reconstruction in conjunction with the changing socio-economical transformations taking place in Beijing, Hong Kong, and Taipei. Adopting the study of language choice as a symbolic creation of self and other within a broader political, economic and historical context will not only give significance to the theoretical paradigm but be seen as significant by the speakers of Chinese.

Implications for the Emerging transnational Chinese Communities

The increasing interactions among speakers of emerging Chinese transnational communities have raised several concerns for the standard Chinese established by the end of the twentieth century. As reported by scholars such as Chen (1999), one of the major goals of language reform in China has long been to achieve the unification of speech and writing, and the replacement of *wenyan* by *baihua* as the base of a standard written code is considered to be a decisive achievement in that direction (p. 114). With national unity achieved, modernization has taken place both in China and Taiwan. The issue of implementing a standard language based on a single locale and that contains features that are not indigenous to outsiders has been proved to be problematic (See Chapter 2 and 3 for Taiwan's situation). For example, in light of China's rapid economic growth and its increasing interactions with people from Hong Kong and Taiwan, Zhang (2005) advocates a cosmopolitan Mandarin, which has been practiced by Beijing professionals. This hybrid Chinese is mixed with features from Hong Kong and Taiwan Mandarin as well as occasional English expressions. Zhang's rationale is derived from practical concerns and is built on the notion of the linguistic market proposed by Bourdieu (1977, 1991). Linguistic features are examined as symbolic resources used by the professionals in foreign businesses to build a new social identity that is not bounded by a territorial matrix (Zhang 2005, p. 432). In addition, Zhang proposes to consider the existence of supra-local or transnational linguistic markets in which a "standard" variety (of a nation-state or a territorially-based community) may not be the "standard" against which values of other varieties are compared and established, and to look beyond the linear dimension of the standard and vernacular in both the description and treatment of variant data (cf. 2005, p. 458).

Along similar lines, Chris Li (2004) points out that a network of standard Chinese has emerged and been practiced by news broadcasters on both sides of the Taiwan Strait. This emerging "network standard Chinese" is devoid of the word-final -erization that is indigenous to Beijing speech, but retains the retroflex initials which most rural Taiwanese speakers lack. Li (2004, p. 128) further concludes that we may be witnessing the rise of a modern Chinese educated accent that cuts across geographical boundaries. The end result may be the development of middle-class urban varieties of Chinese that are generally much more similar to one another all across China than they are to the local working-class or rural varieties.

The language situation in Taiwan can be seen as a tale of national imagination or re-imagination during waves of nationalism, democracy and multiculturalism. With culture, nation and language entangled and history constantly reinterpreted for emerging identity locally and globally, juggling between different languages is comparable to acts of identity. In the following chapters, we will take up some of the crucial issues in the odyssey of this quest for identity and the agony of a language choice. Chapter 2 will lay the groundwork of language choices in Taiwan, with its first part introducing a functional analysis and the second part pointing out a promising approach to language choice found in political oratory.

Notes

1. The smoothness of *jing youzi* (Beijing naives who are smooth and streetwise) extends to a stereotypical speech style, known as *youzi huashe* (oily mouth smooth tongue) or *youqiang huadiao* (oily accent smooth tune). Both expressions mean "glib" or "having the gift of gab." They also refer to the particular sound of Beijing speech. This is what is known among lay people, both locals and non-Beijingers, as the "heavy r-sounding" feaure (Zhang 2005, p. 441).
2. The change from one language to another in a discourse is better understood in the linguistic literature as code-switching. According to Monica Heller, this language phenomenon is so prominent that even those who switch codes can be unaware of their behavior and may vigorously deny doing anything of the kind (Heller 1988, p. 1).
3. The term symbolic capital is from Pierre Bourdieu (1977) who uses it to refer to non-material resources that are socially valued within a community, such as honor, reputation, good breeding, or talent.
4. This chapter focuses on the word final retroflexations termed -erization by Barnes (1977) which occur frequently in Northern Chinese speech.
5. See Chapter 4 for more details on the meaning of becoming Taiwanese.
6. Following Rabinow, the notion of self described here is defined as ". . . neither the purely cerebral *cogito* of the Cartesians, nor the deep psychological self of the Freudians. Rather, it is the culturally mediated and historically situated self which finds itself in a continuously changing world of meaning (Rabinow 1977, p. 1)."
7. Since 1955, the People's Republic of China's term for the common language based on the northern dialects with Beijing pronunciation as the norm (Norman 1988, p. 135).
8. This was abolished in 1905.
9. Public planning of language questions in China goes back at least as far as 213 B.C. with the unification of characters undertaken by Li Si as part of Qin Shi Huang's unification of China (Lehmann 1975, p. 42).
10. There are differences between Min, Southern Min, and Tai-yu, mostly due to circumstances of language contact and the latter's colonial experience with Japan. However, we are only focusing on the language situation in Taiwan and thus are using Tai-yu throughout this book.
11. The Romanization for Cantonese in this chapter follows Professor Parker Pok-fei Huang's system.
12. According to *The Basic Law* for Hong Kong as Special Administrative Region of the PRC, Chapter 1, Article 9 states, "In addition to the Chinese language, English may also be used as an official language by the executive authorities, legislative, and judiciary." The article does not spell out what which variety of the Chinese language is referred to, though in reality, most people speak Cantonese as their first language and use it in most of their daily life situations.
13. Notably, Dutch missionaries in the seventeenth century first introduced Romani-

zation in order to help aboriginal people convert to Christianity, to read to them and translate for them the Bible, and to write contracts.

14. See Chapters 3 and 4 for a fuller account of the sociopolitical ramifications of these issues.

15. Readers are reminded again of the arbitrariness and the symbolic power of a linguistic sign (which is the focus of this chapter). Not all people arriving in Taiwan from China in the late 1940s, especially those not from the northern parts, had the -erization. Nevertheless, the example is given to highlight the hypersensitivities generated by political tensions.

16. I am grateful to Professor Fred C. Blake for sharing this insight with me (personal communication).

17. The teaching of -erization is an unresolved issue. Barnes (1977) points out that it is the plain Mandarin (a variety devoid of -erization) that should be recommended to students. He states that foreign speakers of plain Mandarin can expect to find their speech widely accepted, but are unlikely to invite amused or perhaps even pejorative reactions on the part of native listeners (1977, p. 225).

18. This and the previous expulsion of Taipei from the UN in 1972 greatly devastated the KMT's legitimacy. Over the years, efforts have been made by both Taiwan and the U.S. to resolve issues by implementing regulations such as the Taiwan Relations Act, through arms sales, and by improving trade and cultural ties. Different administrations have interpreted these matters differently. At times, things look calm and peaceful as business across the Taiwan Strait booms; yet, at other times, incidents such as Taiwan political figure Lee Teng-hui's visit to his U.S. alma mater Cornell University in 1995 can provoke both diplomatic and military standoffs between the U.S. and the PRC. Since 1995 Taiwan's economy has sagged, but Lee won unprecedented support and in 1996 became the first directly elected president in Chinese history. For a fuller account of the volatile situation, see Richard Bush and Michael E. O'Hanlon. 2007. *A War Like No Other: The Truth About China's Challenge to America*. Hoboken, New Jersey; John Wiley & Sons, Inc.

Chapter 2
Language Choice in Mandarin and Tai-yu

Introduction

In Taiwan a person's alternating among languages such as Mandarin, Tai-yu, and, to a lesser extent, English can be seen as a way to profile one's group memberships, signaling much of the overall value system of the society—things such as status, solidarity, and professionalism. In the sociolinguistic literature, relating the meaning of language shifts to pre-determined social categories has received much attention, though representative examples are not often taken from Taiwanese contexts. In addition, other than reflecting pre-existing social relations and values, alternating between different languages can be used for political and strategic ends, such as escaping responsibility for a problem or imputing base things to one's adversaries. In view of the lack of representative works on language choice in Tai-yu and the often ingenious use of language by sparring politicians, we devote this chapter to representative works on codeswitching in Taiwan, both from socio-pragmatic and political contexts.

The second chapter aims to provide a general survey of previous studies on codeswitching in Taiwan, with a focus in the first place on the most researched area—the socio-pragmatic aspects of codeswitching—and in the second place on a less known but increasingly important area, the socio-political aspects of codeswitching. With regard to socio-pragmatics, we will note findings on how codeswitching may function as a communicative strategy and how the mixing of official or non-official languages in different types of discourse may fulfill various functions such as reported speech, topic qualification, solidarity, ethnic identity, professionalism and humor. With regard to the socio-political, we will note findings on the use of codeswitching as an interpersonal strategy, where boundaries can be drawn, negotiated and lifted by way of using one language or the other. We adopt rational base models, namely the Markedness Model and Rational Choice models, following Myers-Scotton (1993) and Myers-Scotton and Bolonyai (2001) to argue that speakers make rational choices when they make linguistic choices in a multi-lingual setting and also that, while most choices reflect conventional expectations of the rights and obligations entailed by a language in that setting, speakers make linguistic choices as individuals. Based on the findings of previous research and additional research by the author, a generalization will be presented as to how codeswitching is used as a communicative strategy to fulfill various socio-pragmatic and political functions in Taiwan and how these functions have evolved over the past two decades as economic changes and democratization have taken hold.

The chapter begins with a sociolinguistic profile of Taiwanese and a sketch of language use and choice in the multilingual society of Taiwan. We then consult important works on codeswitching to provide a theoretical orientation, followed by a general survey of previous studies on codeswitching in Taiwan. Major findings of these studies, especially concerning the functions of and motivations for codeswitching in domains such as political campaigns, are further highlighted. Finally, we consider how codeswitching as a conversational strategy and an interpersonal strategy can help achieve various socio/pragmatic/political purposes in general, and how the study of codeswitching can contribute to our understanding of issues of ethnic identity, language policy and language change in particular. In addition, we point out that with increasing numbers of graduate students taking an interest in code choice and code mixing phenomena on the Internet or through computer mediated communication, a new sub-field of codeswitching is emerging, thus highlighting the need for more attention.

The Sociolinguistic Setting in Taiwan

Taiwan is a multilingual community. Mandarin and Tai-yu are the two majority languages, while Hakka, Austronesian and other Chinese dialects are the minority languages. Although there are monolingual speakers, the majority of people in Taiwan today are bilingual in Mandarin and Tai-yu. Alternation between these two languages in daily speech is a prevalent phenomenon.

According to survey information released by the Taiwan government, the Han are the largest ethnic group in Taiwan, comprising roughly 98 percent of the population. The Han in Taiwan are usually classified into two different groups: descendants of early Han Chinese immigrants, and immigrants and their offspring who moved to Taiwan with the Kuomintang (KMT) government in 1945, generally referred to as "mainlanders." The early Han settlers can be further subdivided into the Hakka, mostly from Guangdong province, and the Southern Min, who are primarily from the southeastern province of Fujian. Today, Taiwan's population is mainly composed of four major ethnolinguistic groups: the

Southern Min (73.3 percent), the Hakka (12 percent), the Mainlanders (13 percent), and the native Austronesians (1.7 percent) (Huang 1993). The Southern Min group's language is often referred to as Tai-yu. Intermarriage among all the groups is quite common, so the distinguishing characteristics of each group are growing fainter with the passage of time (Huang 1993; P. Chen 1999).

The rising status and popularity of Tai-yu and other non-Mandarin languages is due partly to the lifting of martial law in 1987. That year the KMT government (1945-2000), among many other changes, ended the ban on other political parties and loosened its control of the printed media, radio, and television programs. Programs aired or printed in languages other than Mandarin were no longer subject to limitations on such things as hours and to ad hoc censorship; the use of non-Mandarin languages in public was no longer punished or restricted. In 1993, the teaching of non-Mandarin languages at the elementary school level began to be encouraged. Interest in learning and teaching non-Mandarin languages rose, and there was considerable discussion of curriculum design and implementations of mother tongue language teaching and English language teaching. As a result, the teaching of English and mother tongue languages was implemented and enforced at all elementary schools nationwide starting in 2001.

In addition, the media played an important role in promoting and reviving Tai-yu and other non-Mandarin languages. With popular Tai-yu programs, songs, and chic phrases constantly appearing in the media, people became more accustomed to the use of Tai-yu in public domains. More and more Taiwanese, especially politicians, attempted to speak Tai-yu in public. Such a drastic turn of language attitude and policy revised the status of non-Mandarin languages, which had been treated as "non-standard" at best and were associated with lower socio-economic status (Berg 1986; M. Y. Chang 1996; Figueroa 1988; Huang 1993, 2000; Tse 2000). Scholars contrasted this new policy with the old one, i.e. exclusive use of the Mandarin language. For example, S. C. Chen (1996a) pointed out that the policy came about as a backlash against the strict imposition of Mandarin Chinese in the past. It was designed to implement mother tongue teaching in schools with the goal of repairing the decay of ethnic languages in Taiwan.

Whereas some people saw the relaxed language policy as an opportunity for the revitalization of non-Mandarin languages, others took a more drastic political stance. Feelings of resentment and inferiority, which had not been visible during the era of the strict Mandarin policy, found an outlet and even a platform. As Tse (2000) stated, there was a trend toward the increased use of local mother tongues as a symbol of defiance against the establishment, as an expression of democratization, as a sign of localism, and as an assertion of ethnolinguistic identity. For quite a long time, language seemed to be a dividing force rather than a unifying one, increasing the social and psychological distance among the major ethnic groups (2000, p. 161).

This, then, has been the situation of the major ethnic groups and languages in Taiwan today. The old language policy enacted and enforced by the KMT beginning in 1945, which adopted an exclusive and restricted attitude toward non-Mandarin varieties, is all but gone. Non-Mandarin varieties are now encouraged, used in public, and taught in school. They have encroached into public domains such as education, politics and the media. Increasing use and mixing of local languages is particularly visible during election campaigns. An ability to use local dialects is regarded as highly appealing. Many indigenous Mainlander candidates have started taking Tai-yu or Hakka lessons, employing speech coaches to help them "speak in tongues" during campaigns. Influenced by the dynamic socio-political changes, codeswitching has come to be a common mode of communication in Taiwan. It not only enriches the linguistic repertoire of the speech community, but also serves as a communicative strategy.

Literature Review

The codeswitching studies done in Taiwan include code alternation between Mandarin and Tai-yu, English and other languages. The present survey deals only with studies on codeswitching between Tai-yu and other languages, mainly Mandarin. These codeswitching studies have been conducted from different perspectives: the syntactic approach (e.g. Cheng 1989), the psycholinguistic approach (e.g. Jian, 2000), the socio-psychological approach (e.g. J. M. Wang 2001), and some from the socio-pragmatic (M.Y. Chang, 1996; S. C. Chang, 2000; Shih and Su 1993; Shih 1995, 1998; Shih and Sung 1998; Su 1994), and socio-political perspective (Shih 1995, 1998; Wei 2001b, Wei 2002). Besides these, there have also been some unpublished papers treating attitude surveys of codeswitching (Chang & Hsu 2002; Q. S. Wang 2003) and the special characteristics of on-line language with codeswitching (Wu 2001; Chen and Lai 2003).

The literature review in the following sections will center on some major works on codeswitching from the socio-pragmatic perspective and the socio-political perspective. It is hoped that through this joint research we can arrive at new insights into the popularity of codeswitching in all forms of discourse, and offer a better explanation of how codeswitching is employed in political discourse to achieve goals such as redefining boundaries, assuming identities, and escaping responsibilities.

Socio-pragmatic Approach to Codeswitching

Codeswitching can be defined as "the use of two or more linguistic varieties in the same conversation or interaction" (Scotton and Ury 1977). A codeswitch might signal several things, and scholars are still debating how and why people codeswitch (Li 1998; Stroud 1992). A socio-pragmatic approach, however, is concerned with questions such as the kinds of functions that can be fulfilled by way of alternating one's languages. As interest in codeswitching takes hold, many scholars have adopted a more positive attitude toward codeswitching and have proposed that a switch of codes might be an unintentional act that is a conventional move to reflect a change of topic, participant, or setting. However, it can also be an indirect language strategy to signal symbolic connotations such as authority, ethnic solidarity or identity, or a strategic tactic to redefine boundaries among speakers (Gal 1998; Heller 1988, 1995; Scotton and Ury 1977).

Blom and Gumperz (1972) first proposed that the functions of codeswitching could be analyzed in terms of situational switching and metaphorical switching. Situational switching occurs when there is a change of participants, settings, or topics. A speaker's change of codes reflects societal norms and the consensus among participants. In contrast, metaphorical switching happens when speakers use a code to convey not only referential meanings but also symbolic connotations such as degree of involvement, objectiveness, or a power struggle. Whereas situational switching reflects the conventional linguistic expectations and usage of a community, metaphorical switching allows speakers to tap into the contextualized meanings of a code in order to convey oblique messages. Gumperz and Hernandez-Chavez (1975) and Gumperz (1982) further propose a variety of rhetorical and stylistic functions for codeswitching. They range from signaling a distinction between direct and reported speech, to marking interjections and providing sentence-fillers, and to clarifying and emphasizing a message.

These findings have influenced many scholarly works, and have inspired and generated many similar works in Taiwan. For example, Kubler (1988) adopts a functional approach toward codeswitching, investigating exchanges between Mandarin and Tai-yu in Taiwan. His study concludes that codeswitching is most common among younger city speakers, and that the reasons for codeswitching include: ease of communication, ensuring complete comprehension on the part of the listener, desire for variety of style, and incomplete proficiency in a particular code (Kubler 1988). His study has generated much interest in codeswitching between Mandarin and Tai-yu in Taiwan. Whereas Kubler did a pioneering study on the exchange between Mandarin and Tai-yu in a single conversation, others have conducted more elaborate surveys and looked into other domains for data and evidence.

Following Kubler's path, others tried to broaden the scope and provided not only larger quantities of data but also tried to solicit attitudes towards codeswitching. Shih and Su (1993) studied the phenomena of code mixing[1] of Mandarin with spoken Tai-yu, and classified the mixed codes according to syntactic, semantic and functional categories. Shih carried out another study in 1995, examining Mandarin as a matrix language and Tai-yu and English as embedded languages, and laying bare the socio-pragmatic functions of the switched codes.

These two studies both adopted quantitative and qualitative methods to survey codeswitching behavior among speakers who constantly mix Tai-yu, Mandarin, and English in daily conversation. The studies drew on large samples from various forms of speech, including public lectures, campaign forum speeches, campaign debates, classroom lectures, television and radio programs, talk shows, parliamentary interpellations, radio commercials, business talks, and daily conversation. In addition to providing a detailed semantic and functional taxonomy, these two studies revealed that people switch to Mandarin or Tai-yu respectively for quite different pragmatic purposes. When people switch from Mandarin to Tai-yu, they most often do so to try to show humor, expressiveness or solidarity. When speakers switch from Tai-yu to Mandarin, they most often do so for the functional effects of message qualification, establishment of authority, eruditeness, direct quotation, or lack of vocabulary. When people switch from Mandarin or Tai-yu to English, they often do so for the sake of professionalism, lack of proper vocabulary or direct quotation. The different socio-pragmatic functions of different languages in codeswitching reflect the social status of the languages, Mandarin and English being the high language and Tai-yu the low language.

Besides the above studies, Shih and Sung (1998) conducted other research on codeswitching in written language. They chose newspaper headlines as the database, because newspapers mirror society better than other forms of written language. Data were collected from three newspapers: the *Central Daily News*, the *Independent Evening Post* and the *China Times*, from 1987 to 1991, just before and after the lifting of political restrictions on newspapers in 1988. Based on Myers-Scotton's (1993) Markedness Model, they found that as a marked choice, code-mixed Tai-yu in newspaper headlines can serve a variety of functions, including humorous effect, expressiveness, poetic effect, commentary, authenticity, solidarity, a touch of local flavor, and attention-getting. Among them, expressiveness, humorous effect, a touch of local flavor and getting attention were the most prominent. They also found a close relationship between language and the socio-political climate. The study reported that from 1987 to 1991 an increased use of code mixing prevailed among all three newspapers, especially in 1989, one year after the political restrictions on newspapers were lifted. The political stance of a particular newspaper was found to have substantial influence on its use of code mixing. For example, the *Central Daily News*, which had a close connection with the ruling KMT, used much less Tai-yu code mixing in its headlines than the other two newspapers.

In addition, questionnaire surveys of readers' attitudes toward code mixing in newspaper headlines as well as interviews with newspaper editors were conducted. The results indicated that the majority of respondents had quite positive attitudes toward the embedding of Tai-yu in newspaper headlines. Overall, the research of Shih and Sung (1998) provided solid grounds for explaining why code mixing of Tai-yu has become popular in Taiwan newspapers.

S. C. Chen (1996b) studied codeswitching patterns in a campus setting and found that codeswitching as a verbal strategy can be adopted to fulfill five social and linguistic functions: the expressive, directive, poetic, metalinguistic, and referential. The results of her study also indicated that code switching has a dynamic relationship to the communicative intent of a speaker. That is, code switching can be adopted as a "we-code" to express group solidarity and as a "they-code" to establish social distance.

In short, most of the socio-pragmatic codeswitching studies in Taiwan have adopted a functional approach and their findings are for the most part consistent with those of major works in the field, namely, that code switching is a universal phenomenon that mostly occurs in diglossic communities where speakers are multilingual and adopt various codes for socio-pragmatic functions.

Socio-political Approach to Codeswitching

Most of the previous codeswitching studies in Taiwan observe that codeswitching fulfills the general functions outlined by Gumperz (1982). Missing, however, is a concrete picture of how the unique linguistic setting of Taiwan and the dialogic socio-political tensions between Mandarin and Tai-yu can contribute to our understanding of the use of codeswitching for political purposes. With the exception of Shih (1995), few studies have looked into language choice and use in political discourse. Shih compares the time allotted to Mandarin and to Tai-yu in the 1994 Taiwan gubernatorial election and Taipei city mayoral election campaign debates and forum lectures, and found that a close relationship between a candidate's choice of language, his or her political background, and the audience he or she is trying to address. The candidates switch codes most often for the purpose of implying their political stance, and for identifying with the ethnic background of the audience.

Early research projects are mostly descriptive in nature. In order to reach a better understanding of why people codeswitch, Wei (2001b; 2002) conducted two in-depth qualitative studies of codeswitching in election campaigning. These studies suggest that the strength of codeswitching lies in its indeterminacy, i.e. strategic ambiguities, which arise from either conventional usage or expectations of a specific code, the rights and obligations among interlocutors, and other factors at play. Speakers switch codes not only to redefine or renegotiate the rules of the interaction, but also to avoid the risk of being put on record (negative politeness), thus escaping obligations, responsibility and even creating involvement in a contested context such as political discourse.

With the end of martial law, the rise of ethnic consciousness, and increasing democratization in Taiwan, scholars have taken note of how a change of language can create discoursal as well strategic effects. For example, Shih (1998) notes that political candidates and campaigners switch among Tai-yu, Mandarin and other ethnic languages to signal mixed ethnic identity. This kind of codeswitching is most likely to occur at openings, greetings and closings where politicians try out as many languages as they can manage in order to include live audiences, viewers and readers across all ethnicities. This kind of emblematic switching can be further combined with the consideration of the setting or broadcast media. For instance, television may broadcast live events at particular locales. Shih (1998) finds that during televised speeches and debates most candidates choose the official language, Mandarin, as their matrix language. The choice of the official language in this context not only helps to ensure understanding for audiences from all ethnic backgrounds, but also lends authority to the candidates' speeches. This identifying oneself with a specific locale via a specific language has become more prevalent during campaigns in which the issue of identity/ethnicity can either make or break the outcome of the election. An accomplished politician can further create an intense sense of ethnicity by using one of the vernaculars and combining it with puns, homonyms or slang. In addition to the scholarship produced by researchers in Taiwan, issues related to shifting identities by way of speaking different languages have also attracted attention from scholars across the Strait. For example, Chen (1999) also takes note of the dynamic sociolinguistic situation in Taiwan and how that can contribute to a recalibration of language and identity:

> Since the late 1980s, there has been an increased awareness of regional identity which, among other things, is most evident in the calls to enhance the status of local dialects. Issues surrounding the use of dialects and modern standard Chinese are highly politicized, with southern-min taken to be a symbol of local identity that separates its speakers from those speaking other Chinese dialects, and for that mater, separates Taiwan from other parts of the Chinese community (p. 61).

To illustrate our point that codeswitching should be treated as an important language strategy in political discourse we will use an example of codeswitching between Mandarin and Tai-yu in President Chen Shui-bian's political campaign during the 2001 legislative races. Codeswitching is important for politicians and for politics because people infer meanings from an act of codeswitching. Since much of the act of inference depends on context, or on the listener's presuppositions and/or expectations of the speaker or issue, the meaning of a codeswitch is at best blurred, and often negotiable. Such indeterminacy works best in a context such as political discourse, where conflicts and contentions are prevalent and where indirectness, i.e. saying one thing but meaning another, is often necessary to protect one's best interests. According to Obeng (1997), political interests and political necessity as well as personal face-saving motivate indirectness (1997, p. 49). The indirectness may also be motivated by politeness (cf. Brown and Levinson 1987) since speakers don't always want to be straightforward, especially when involved in sensitive issues or when having to face complicated consequences. Other than escaping obligations and responsibilities, speakers can also adopt indirectness to achieve the sense of involvement that comes from being understood without saying what one means (Lakoff 1979). Tannen (1989) further argues that by requiring the listener or reader to fill in unstated meanings, indirectness contributes to a sense of involvement through mutual participation in sense making (1989, p. 23). Scholars such as Obeng (1997), Chilton and Ilyin (1993), and Masci and Semino (1996) have studied indirect features such as allusions, metaphors, circumlocutions, and innuendos and analyzed their pragmatic and strategic functions in political discourse. Wei (2001a) studied the allusions and metaphors in Taiwanese political campaigns used in major election campaign discourses since 1996. Her study demonstrates that allusions and metaphors are among the most prevalent linguistic strategies in Taiwanese political discourse. Nevertheless, codeswitching in political discourse receives relatively little attention. It is thus time to turn our attention to the examples and contributions codeswitching can make for the study of political discourse specifically, and for sociolinguistics generally.

Example and Analysis

In the following example, we will see how codeswitching can help a politician escape taking responsibility for something. Symbolic acts of identity can be made by choosing a language, which entails a group membership that either includes or excludes the speaker, and exemption can be achieved by tapping into the unofficial status of a vernacular and by adopting a different voice. A skilled politician can thus temporarily transform himself from policy maker into innocent victim. The example is as follows:

> Zhonghua Renmin Gongheguo burang women miaoli lizizhen qu, *chit8-tiuN1 ho2-pai5 pian3-seng5 a-piN2-ah beh4 lia7-khi3 tai5, chin1 u7 chha7 hia1 che7?* (Miaoli campaigning, responding to the criticism over Chen's APEC representative handling, 10/27/01 Era News)

Trans: the PRC (People's Republic of China) won't let our Miaoli adviser Li attend (APEC). A good card was turned into A-bian's capital punishment. Did it really make that much difference?

In this example, Chen was responding to criticisms over his handling of China's rejection of Chen's appointed candidate, Li Yuan-Cu, a retired former vice-president, as the ROC representative to the 21st APEC (Asia-Pacific Economic Cooperation) Summit, held in Shanghai. Because of pressure from Beijing, Taiwan's choice of an APEC representative was supposed to be restricted to a cabinet minister or business leader (06/06/01, CNN Asia Edition). Chen's choice of Li was considered by Beijing as inappropriate because Li was not a business leader and because of his "official" status as a former vice-president (10/14/01 BBC News). Chen decided to ignore this rejection and declined to send an alternative representative. The opposition parties, however, interpreted Chen's handling of the issue as playing up the antagonism between Beijing and Taipei at the expense of Taiwan's economic future in order to raise his and the DPP's popularity for the 2001 December election (10/21/01 *China Times* (Taipei)).

Given this context, Chen's choice of a marked language, i.e. Mandarin at the beginning of his speech, was loaded with ambiguities. On the one hand, it could serve as an indirect quotation of what had been publicized in the media about the rejection of his APEC representative by the Chinese authorities. On the other hand, Mandarin here could function as the "they" code—the language of the Chinese authorities who rejected the Taiwanese APEC representative and/or the language of the opposition parties who had been criticizing the president on this issue. The point is that it is precisely these creative ambiguities and indeterminacy of readings that makes a skillful language user and intensifies the strength of codeswitching in a complex and contested discourse such as politics.

In the second part of the example, Chen switched to Tai-yu. The ambiguities here are that his switch to Tai-yu, the vernacular language, the language of the DPP and the unmarked language in the locale, can be interpreted as message qualification, or an act of playfulness because of the paired rhyming of the two Tai-yu phrases, "ho2- pai5" (good card) and "tai" (to kill). Moreover, we can argue that, under the framework of the Rational Choice model, Chen is calculating his gains and losses in choosing either Mandarin or Tai-yu, where each choice entails roles such as the president, a member of the DPP, someone who is innocent or someone who just wants to be one of the people. With each role, certain responsibilities and obligations follow accordingly. Given the contested context of the issue, Chen's choice of Tai-yu, with its unofficial status and its symbolic association with solidarity and camaraderie, not only bails him out of a tough situation, exonerating him from taking responsibility as a policy maker, but also instantly transforms him into an innocent victim who has been taking quite a beating in the media. Chen's last utterance, "Does it really make that much difference?" in Tai-yu further attests to his attempts to minimize the charge over the APEC candidate issue and to maximize his advantage. In sum, his switch to Tai-yu is ambiguous but such ambiguities are well calculated and rationally based, given the contested nature of the context and the risks and responsibility Chen has to face if an alternative choice is made. Chen's choice of Tai-yu, interpreted under the Rational Choice model, depends on his estimation of what choices offer him the greatest benefit, a linguistic move which reflects his goal to enhance his interpersonal relationship with his supporters, increase psychological rewards (i.e. transforming himself from policy maker to an innocent victim), and decrease costs (i.e. minimizing the chances for being interrogated on the issue). The Rational Choice model further sheds light on the speaker's ability to employ a marked choice to purse a complex set of goals and maintain multiple role relationships (Bolonyai and Myers-Scotton 2001, p. 20).

Summary and Conclusion

This chapter has surveyed some of the major recent works on codeswitching in order to argue that codeswitching has been used as a very important interpersonal strategy in Taiwanese daily experience. It also looks into examples in an often-neglected area—political discourse—and argues that codeswitching has been used, at least by some of the more prominent politicians in Taiwan, such as President Chen Shui-bian, as a vital communication strategy to achieve personal and/or political goals.

By reviewing research of the last two decades, we have shown the change in functional uses of and attitudes towards codeswitching in Taiwan, and the ways in which codeswitching has become prevalent in the socio-pragmatic area, as well as its increasing importance in the political realm. Data and results are drawn from oral and written media, and conclusions are made in accordance with the general trends in the field. The act of codeswitching in daily linguistic transactions has become more popular and dynamic since the lifting of martial law in 1987, the lifting of political restrictions on newspapers in 1988, and the increasing ease of vernacular use in public domains. In addition, the incorporation of mother language instruction into the Nine-year Curriculum in 2001 is supporting a variety of languages by direct instruction in schools. An island-wide survey of language attitudes toward codeswitching is needed in the future to test people's acceptance of codeswitching involving English, Japanese and local languages in Taiwan. Aside from some sporadic attitude surveys appearing in some papers (e.g. J. M. Wang 2001; Shih and Sung 1998) and in some unpublished manuscripts (e.g. Chang and Hsu 2002; Q. S. Wang 2003), no systematic and large-scale survey studies have been done in this area. From these surveys, it is clear that the use of Tai-yu or the mixing of Tai-yu with Mandarin used to be looked down upon as a sign of a lack of language proficiency or of emphasizing an ethnic identity. However, it has now evolved from a marked choice to an unmarked choice in most domains, even domains as formal as the president's public speeches or campaign debates. Local ethnic languages used to be used in informal domains and served as a symbol of ethnic identity, but young people now treat a switch to Tai-yu more as a humorous and expressive strategy than as an ethnic symbol. On the other hand politicians have been extensively adopting codeswitching more for the purpose of showing respect and solidarity with the ethnic group being addressed.

During a television campaign, candidates will often switch between Mandarin and local languages in an attempt to send a message of multi-ethnic identity.

This may have to do with the emergence of a new supra-ethnic identity, that of "New Taiwanese,"[2] wherein many Taiwanese have come to identify themselves with the land in which they live, rather than making reference to where their ancestors came from. With increasing democratization, Tai-yu and other ethnic languages are taking up more of the public domain, including politics, education and the media. Mixing Tai-yu with other languages and alternating various language choices have become all the more prevalent in mundane conversations and popular among politicians in public discourse.

From the survey of codeswitching studies and the review of socio-political changes in Taiwan, we have observed a change in language choice over the past two decades—from clear domains of official language and vernacular languages to the versatile mixing and switching of languages in almost all domains. In this study we first focused our attention on the descriptive analyses of the socio-pragmatic functions of codeswitching, and then on how individuals, especially politicians, manipulate the ambiguities of codeswitching and use them either for boundary-making or as a boundary-leveling strategy in a contested context. The widespread increase of codeswitching in Taiwan reflects not only the dynamism of language and politics but also a pragmatism among young people who see themselves living in a harmonious multi-ethnic and multilingual society.

Implications

This chapter has provided a review of the research on codeswitching in Taiwan from both socio-pragmatic and socio-political contexts. With the rapid socio/economic/political changes that Taiwan has undergone, alternating between languages has become a common practice not just among college students and in newspaper headlines but also among aspiring politicians. The socio-pragmatic aspects of language alternation are tracked by the correlation/variation model (Fishman, 1965; 1972; Gumperz and Hernandez-Chavez, 1975; Gumper 1982), and the results in general reflect an array of social values such as humor, objectivity, professionalism, and solidarity. It will be interesting to see if other multilingual Chinese communities also demonstrate such language patterns. One pertinent case in point is the situation in some of the special economic zones in China, such as Shenzhen. As in Taiwan, rapid economic growth and increasing contacts between people speaking different regional varieties of Chinese there have provided a vital impetus for language alternation. Though Shenzhen, unlike Taiwan, has not experienced the kind of democratization pressures causing people to demand rights and representation via language, and although issues such as increasing demands for mother tongue education and written representation for Chinese varieties other than Mandarin have not received much attention yet, it will be interesting to see if a relaxed language policy is ever tried in Shenzhen, whereupon concerns and decisions based on consensus and integration might help bring out these issues.

In addition, in both Taiwan and Shenzhen, the media have played important roles in facilitating and sustaining the constant use of language alternation. Bilingual (Mandarin/Tai-yu or Mandarin/Cantonese) television and radio programs are the meeting grounds for multilingual speakers. According to Zhang (2005), "While the increasing economic link with other parts of China has given impetus to the use of Putonghua, the rising economic status of Guangdong province and the increasing business connections with Hong Kong [have] also raised the status of Cantonese, the dialect of both the provincial capital and the then British colony" (ibid, pp. 358-59). The availability of Cantonese radio and television programs, including those from Hong Kong received in Shenzhen, provides an opportunity for migrants, especially well-educated intellectuals from the north, to learn Cantonese. At the same time, non-Putonghua speakers are also exposed to the standard dialect through Putonghua programs. For many people, especially the young, the ability to speak Putonghua is associated with culture and good education while the ability to speak Cantonese is regarded as trendy and fashionable (ibid, also in Fu, 1999a, 1999b).

The socio-political aspect of language choice and use in this chapter is inspired by works of Myers-Scotton, C. and Ury, W. (1977) and Myers-Scotton (1993, 2001). In these studies language alternation signifies a set of rights and responsibilities during interaction. However, there are other influential approaches to codeswitching such as "conversational analysis" (CA) (Auer, 1984, 1988; Li, W. and Milroy, L. 1995, 1998, 2002) in which the researcher relies on sequential analysis of the data to verify a set of social rules and categories in play. According to Li (1998), "Those who adopt the CA approach to codeswitching argue that we must not assume that, in any given conversation, speakers switch languages in order to 'index' speaker identity, attitudes, power relations, formality, etc.; rather, we must be able to demonstrate how such things as identity, attitude and relationship are presented, understood, accepted or rejected, and changed in the process of interaction" (1998, p. 163). Our concern is that much of the salience between the tensions of micro/macro factors depends on the type of data one collects. In the case of the socio-pragmatic codeswitching work provided in the first part of the chapter, most of the data are single utterances, and the socio-political codeswitching work is a monologue from a single politician. As such, it might not be feasible to look into sequential interaction for local meaning or negotiation. Instead, rather than looking for a definitive local meaning of a choice of language, which might connect with identity, attitude or a power relationship, the real strength of switching between languages in political discourse, as presented in the above example, might lie in dynamic socio-political contexts which give complex meanings, or in multiple social roles of the switch. As we have demonstrated with the example, ambiguities, and indeterminacy serve both pragmatic and political purposes. Here, "macro" factors such as socio-political changes override our concerns for "micro" factors, the sequential interactions among speakers in breaking new grounds for codeswitching research in a domain that is relatively underexplored. In addition, we did incorporate the social background and checked our analysis against it. It will be interesting to use the CA model to compare examples from politicians speaking to each other in order to verify some of claims we make in this chapter.

In the next chapter, we will turn our attention to one aspiring politician, Chen Shui-bian, using more of his political oratory as a case study in how making choices between Mandarin and Tai-yu can enable political maneuvering. That is, with language high on the agenda during elections, winning voters from different constituencies is crucial for making or breaking a race. Attracting votes, appeasing foes, blaming others, and imputing scandal to opponents are all part of the election game. A careful study of how Mandarin and Tai-yu are incorporated in rhetoric will reveal how symbolic identity can be enacted, negotiated, and rejected.

Notes

1. There have been debates in the codeswitching literature on the difference between codeswitching and code mixing. In the papers of Shih and Su (1993) and Shih and Sung (1998), "code mixing" is adopted in place of codeswitching because the database for these researches consists of single sentences and the alternation of language choices only occurs intra-sententially. In the present study, however, codeswitching is used as a cover term for both codeswitching and code mixing phenomena.

2. See Chapter 4 for further detailed discussion.

Chapter 3
Chen Shui-bian's Language Choices

Introduction

In this chapter, language choice is seen as more than an enactment of social values or a problem of categories. Instead, the issue is dealt with from the viewpoint of an ever important but often neglected topic, political discourse. We focus our attention on the campaign speeches of one of the most prominent politicians in present day Taiwan—the president, Chen Shui-bian. As Taiwan experienced economic growth in the 1980s, increasing demands for democratization brought to the forefront issues such as ethnic consciousness. The increasing use of Tai-yu by the president, as well as other non-official languages though to a much lesser degree, combined with the fact that the languages were used in public domains such as politics and media events, not only helped raise the visibility but also the status of Tai-yu, which had been seen not only as "the language of Taiwan" by active pro-independence supporters but also as "the language of the people" by "ethnic Taiwanese."[1] That kind of ethnic boundary breaking/making via a language choice in the political and media arenas can be seen as an interesting case of codeswitching to illustrate how ethnic identities can be enacted and negotiated through language choices.

We adopt Rational Choice (RC) models (e.g. Myers-Scotton 1993; Myers-Scotton and Bolonyai 2001) to analyze Chen's codeswitching in political discourse, and argue that although most of the instances of his codeswitching reflect conventional expectations of language choice to a certain extent, a speaker such as Chen definitely can be counted on to make rational, individual choices. This is especially evident in light of tensions between Taiwan's interest groups and the many attacks Chen sustains on heated issues. In addition, Chen, like most politicians, relies on ambiguities inferred from language choice to avoid taking responsibility for problems, to redefine interpersonal boundaries, and to take refuge in more positive roles. In short, a Rational Choice-based model helps explain how a politician can use an array of language choices to maximize personal/political gains while minimizing personal/political risks.

We further suggest that the inference of a codeswitching is indeterminate and ambiguous (Heller 1988). The ambiguity and indeterminacy of a language choice are especially important in political discourse where conflicts and confrontations are common and where indirectness yet involvement are necessary. Thus, studying codeswitching in political discourse will on the one hand enhance our understanding of codeswitching in general from the perspective of a specific genre, and on the other hand will add to our appreciation of political discourse from a more specific sociolinguistics point of view.

In the first part of the chapter, we outline the theoretical framework by reviewing Gumperz (1982a), Heller (1988) and Myers-Scotton (1976) as well as the accommodation theory and theories on indirectness. The second section provides an account of modern Taiwan's increasing democratization and the impact of that trend on language use and language alternation. The third section is on Chinese politicians' language use in general followed by a short introduction of Chen Shui-bian. The chapter closes first with an examination of texts and discussions followed by conclusions and implications for further studies.

Theoretical Frames

Following Gumperz (1982a), Heller (1988), and Myers Scotton (1976), we treat codeswitching not only as a social mechanism of negotiation and definition of social roles, networks, and boundaries (Heller 1988, p.1), but also propose that codeswitching be treated as an important but often ignored verbal strategy in political discourse, a strategy which allows one to achieve pragmatic and strategic functions without assuming the responsibility or taking the risk of being put on record. The question we ask is how a speaker, especially a skilled politician, given conflicting demands in the context, can use different languages to perform a set of obligations and at the same time avoid responsibility for what he says, or even interrogation, simply by the inference of a chosen code. Indeed, the indeterminacy of an inference drawn from a language choice is crucial since it is often generated beyond the semantic content of the sequential sentences and arises from conflicting expectations of interest groups. Moreover, an inference from an instance of codeswitching can be achieved non-conventionally, i.e. by way of humor, slang, or analogy. In sum, much of what codeswitching can achieve as a conversational strategy, apart from the conventional meanings of a code, is derived from making inferences, which are further dependent on the context and the shared understanding and expectations of the interlocutors.

Thus, by studying codeswitching in a political context, we are able to see how allegations are made or disclaimed, boundaries created or destroyed, and responsibilities assumed or avoided.

Functional Approach to Codeswitching

Blom and Gumperz (1972) propose the terms "situational switching" and "metaphorical switching" to incorporate two types of language alternation. Situational codeswitching is used to refer to the Fishman type of domain analysis, i.e. participants, settings, or topics, while metaphorical codeswitching is used to refer to symbolic connotations, such as intimacy and objectivity. Gumperz and Hernandez-Chavez (1975) and Gumperz (1982) further propose a variety of rhetorical and stylistic functions of codeswitching. These range from signaling a distinction between direct and reported speech, to marking interjections and providing sentence-fillers, to clarifying and emphasizing a message through codeswitched reiteration of utterance, and to qualifying a message or structuring information. These findings have influenced many scholarly works, not a few of which have offered similar accounts of the types of functions of codeswitching. For example, Auer (1995) suggests that the juxtaposition of codes entails the juxtaposition of two semiotic systems; these can also be seen as (at least) two different ways of organizing a world view of symbolic and material resources and cultural, economic, and political practices. Heller (1995) offers similar accounts and states that the juxtaposition of codes illuminates the relationship between institutional relations of power and those connected to forms of social organization in the broader society (Heller 1995, p. 374).

Apart from explaining when and how speakers switch between languages, other scholars have tried to account for why codeswitching occurs. Scotton and Ury (1977), for example, reason that the act of codeswitching is a gesture to redefine identity boundaries or a calculation of the rights and obligations of the speaker. They state that a speaker switches codes for either of the two following reasons: to redefine the interaction as appropriate to a different social arena, or to avoid, through continual codeswitching, defining the interaction in terms of any specific social arena. Codeswitching back and forth reflects the speaker's uncertainty concerning which social arena is the best ground on which to carry out the interaction with a view to the speaker's long term and short-term goals (1977, p. 6). Scotton (1972) suggests that when codeswitching occurs in intragroup exchanges, it can be best explained as a mechanism of the negotiation of respective rights and obligations of participants (1972, p. 433). In sum, the above works provide a framework to study language alternation as they are related to social values, and to the rights and obligations associated with different languages.

The Speech Accommodation Theory

In the Speech Accommodation Theory (SAT) proposed by Giles and Smith (1979), linguistic convergence is defined as a strategy whereby speakers adapt to another's communicative behavior in order to gain social approval. Linguistic convergence can further be classified into two types: upward convergence and downward convergence (Giles and Powesland, 1975). A move toward a high variety is upward convergence, whereas a move toward a low variety is downward convergence. There are also occasions where speakers perform excess convergence for various pragmatic purposes, thus causing over-accommodation. SAT is important in providing some account of why speakers switch languages in a particular setting. They do so either to gain approval from the audience or to signal disapproval. As for the case of over-accommodation, we observe that some election campaigners who are neither fluent nor familiar with a particular code will strive to make a show of it, which often results in their making fools of themselves, at least temporarily, for the sake of gaining approval or in an attempt to break an ethnic boundary.

Codeswitching as an Indirect Speech Feature in Political Discourse

As we mentioned in the previous section, one of the great advantages of adopting codeswitching, apart from its being a useful conversational strategy where effective discoursal and rhetorical effects can be achieved, lies in strategic ambiguities. The indeterminacy of a codeswitch can arise from several areas, and since neither the speaker nor the hearer can be a total authority on exactly what a code really means in a given context, the meaning of a codeswitch is negotiated indirectly in most cases. Speakers can tap into such semantic polyphony, adopting it for practical and political purposes. Because of the indeterminacy of the inference of an instance of codeswitch, we propose that it should be treated as an important indirect speech feature and that it should be assigned a status equal to other oblique speech features such as allusions and metaphors, able like them to contribute importantly to political communication.

Democratization and Language Use

Alternating between different languages can be a benign linguistic exercise to carry out ordinary social functions such as creating humor, expressing intimacy and showing professionalism. In other contexts, where the values and ideologies of a language are undergoing constant changes as a result of a heightened sense of ethnic pride and consciousness, language choice and alternation can carry out more strategic functions. In order to understand the driving forces behind the prevalent practice of codeswitching in the Taiwanese political scene, it is essential to look at Taiwan's democratization progress first. Moreover, in order to explain the importance of studying the codeswitching practice of a politician, we need to look closely at the individual's repertoires and to ask the question why such an ingenuous skill is available to some but not others. Further, we need to address the issue of why codeswitching is a relatively mild social practice in some Chinese communities such as Shenzhen (cf. implications in Chapter 2) while in others, such as Taiwan, it has taken on acute political connotations in specific historical moments and circumstances. Lastly, we must provide an account of how language choice between Mandarin and Tai-yu can symbolize a power struggle between competing interest groups. That is to say, we must explain how, as ethnic pride and consciousness arose, non-Mandarin dialects became the preferred choices of aspiring politicians intent on challenging the status and authority of Mandarin to win favor with voters and carry various elections.

Historically, KMT rule in Taiwan following the Japanese occupation (1895-1945) didn't get off to an easy start either for the Taiwan people or for the many military families and personnel who came to the island with the KMT, some as early as 1945. On the mainland, the conflict between the CCP and the KMT dragged on, and by 1948 a dire outcome for the KMT was becoming evident. Exhaustion, mismanagement of funds and personnel, and failed economic and political policies all contributed to the KMT's rapid loss of power and representation in China. As Spence (1990) put it: "On the surface the most urgent aspect of the crisis facing the Guomindang[2] was the steady loss of territory in the north to the Communists, and the attendant erosion of the morale of the Nationalist armies. But equally important was the growth of inflation in China, which wrecked all attempts of Chiang Kai-shek and his advisers to reinstitute viable central control (p. 498)." More particularly, Spence (1990) describes the rout of the KMT on the mainland and the victory of the CCP as follows:

> War's end in 1945 found the Guomindang demoralized by the long years of fighting, and its government weakened by personal conflicts and the serious inflation that affected the areas under its control. The party moved swiftly but ineptly to reestablish its control over the former Japanese-held areas, lacking the trained personnel to fill vacant positions and without money to rebuild a war-shattered society. The Communists, also without resources, moved swiftly to seize what areas they could from the defeated Japanese and to secure a firm base of support among the people of north China. The Communists looked particularly to Manchuria as a promising location to build up their military forces for a final assault on Chiang kai-shek. Their strategy was proved correct. By 1948 Chiang's forces in Manchuria

were routed, and his own power base in China proper completely eroded by a now catastrophic inflation and by the defection from his side of majority of China's intellectuals, students, professional classes, and urban workers. During 1949 his remaining forces simply disintegrated, and late that year, as Chiang retreated with his surviving supporters to Taiwan, Mao Zedong in Peking declared the founding of the new People's Republic of China (p. 438).

In comparison, the post World War II transition period for Japanese officials leaving Taiwan was relatively "easier" given a prevailing underlying sense of duty and morality among citizens and government. For the first three months after Japan's formal surrender to the Allies on September 2, 1945, a sense of law and order persisted (Chang 2003, p. 44). The Japanese government allowed Taiwanese elites and civic associations to take more responsibility for maintaining social order, and there was little sign of chaos despite the rapid downturn of the economy and a power vacuum (ibid).

Both the KMT and the people on Taiwan were dealing with much uncertainty. Despite conflicting expectations from both sides and influences from a fifty year Japanese rule, a peaceful and cooperative relationship between Japanese and Taiwanese, that is between the colonial masters and their subjects, distinguished Taiwan from other places such as Korea. On the other hand, greater impediments existed for the KMT. The officials were in the process of losing a civil war to their mainland counterparts. They adhered to a sense of duty and morality inspired by extreme Chinese nationalism and patriotism of a sort that, by the late 1940s, viewed the Taiwan take-over as transitional to the KMT's eventual return and triumph on the mainland. Few were sure how long the transition would take, and serious plans to continue the island's development didn't come until decades later.

Language differences were one of the main obstacles to KMT success in Taiwan, along with false expectations and failed policies. Japanese had been used as the island's official language for many decades, and this public medium was now banned as a result of regime change.[3] Learning modern Chinese (standardized but mainly based on the northern dialect) was enforced in public and at schools and proved especially difficult for those speaking Tai-yu, Hakka or aboriginal languages as mother tongues, since the linguistic diversities were greater for these speakers and since many of them (in their 20s and older) had learned Japanese as their "national language" before the advent of the KMT administration. The linguistic transitions might not have been so difficult for those who came from the mainland at that time, since their regional dialects usually were closer to the Mandarin variety and they didn't have to experience as dramatic a language shift—from Japanese to Chinese—as their Taiwanese counterparts. The KMT believed that enforcing monolingual and Sino-centric language and cultural policies could help consolidate diverging ethnic consciousness and rid the people of Japanese colonial influences, but some of the stringent measures taken by the KMT authorities, such as the banning of languages other than Mandarin and the imposition of martial law (1949), exacerbated clashes and class divisions between the people and their new rulers. There were other issues, too—for example, with the advent of the KMT the allocation of jobs and education was also to a certain degree dependent on ties with KMT officialdom. Consequently, some came to see the KMT government as less caring and competent than the Japanese administration and not genuine in its condescending attitude toward the locals as well as its fixation on "returning to the motherland." These sentiments became seeds of determined opposition even though the sociopolitical climate was made harsh and political radicals were seen as traitors, subject to severe punishments. (See Chapter 4 for more discussion on Taiwanese national consciousness.)

The lifting of martial law in 1987 finally liberated opposition forces. The power of the opposition political parties, notably the Democratic Progressive Party (DPP), rose. The DPP was the most influential opposition group. It was first organized in 1983 by a group of independents professing grassroots sentiments and propagating ideas such as democracy and sovereignty as opposed to authoritarianism and unification. The DPP participated in the 1989 legislative and local elections, which were the first to allow non-KMT members to participate. The party gradually established its power and influence from the grass roots up, and soon was enjoying a steady stream of successes, gaining increasing support and eventually becoming the most powerful opposition party. With Chen Shui-bian winning the year 2000 presidential election, the DPP transformed itself into the ruling party.

Opposition politicians discovered that the choice of which language to use could be a political act. In the legislature, they took to questioning government officials in Tai-yu, knowing that some of the bureaucrats could not understand, simply to embarrass them (*Economist* August 7, 1993). The Taiwan dissidents supporting the DPP pushed for official acceptance of Tai-yu, Hakka, and indigenous languages (cf. Lin 2002). Others advocated making English the second official language for its international status and for pragmatic purposes. Independence minded critics referred to Tai-yu as the "national language" and to Mandarin as the "Beijing dialect" (cf. Erbaugh 1995, p.85). According to Huang (2000), some of the DPP activists saw the KMT's legitimization of Mandarin as the national language as having placed them at a serious disadvantage and in the category of second-class citizens vis-à-vis the mainlanders, who were already enjoying hegemony in the political sphere (2000, p.145). Erbaugh (1995) also states that Taiwan activists today show exquisite sensitivity to mainland policy and use it to goad the Taiwan government toward greater tolerance of and support for both Chinese dialects and indigenous languages. At the same time, miscellaneous trends and forces, especially increasing pride in local culture and an economic boom in southern China, advanced dialect bilingualism more effectively than policy ever could (ibid, p.79). In addition, the speaking of Tai-yu became the prerequisite for candidates seeking to mobilize voters and win elections. Even candidates not speaking Tai-yu as their mother tongue started trying to use it during election campaigns rather than risk being seen as "not one of the people" and, thus, election losers.

Language Use and Symbolic Power

Using Tai-yu or other Chinese languages as a potent tool to identify with the people is no privilege of DPP members. Revolutionaries such as Mao and Deng Xiaoping always took pride in their heavy local accents, and many influential Chinese politicians including Jiang Zemin and Zhu Rongji were fluent in more than one local tongue and used them to identify with the locals. Thanks to the relaxing of attitudes toward language policy in Taiwan since the late 1980s and because of increasing democratization, many non-DPP members either hired speech coaches or otherwise demonstrated that they were making genuine efforts to learn non-standard tongues. Chang Hsiao-yen, grandson of Chiang Kai-shek; James Soong, a former Taiwan governor; and Ma Ying-jeou, former Justice Minister and Mayor of Taipei (1998-2006), all made well publicized efforts to speak, or at least to study, non-Mandarin languages. Their fluency and proficiency might never match that of native speakers such as Lee Teng-hui and Chen Shui-bian, champions in using Taiwanese local idioms and slang, but in other languages including English they showed skill, and their efforts in Tai-yu won them sympathy and support.

The choice between Mandarin and Tai-yu certainly became a strategic one when it came to political interests. Tse (2000) observes that during the 1996 presidential and vice-presidential races, all four vice-presidential candidates spoke Mandarin, though their political stances ranged from ultimate reunification to eventual separatism. Their choice of Mandarin in a public domain such as television debates reflected their intentions to win votes and to get their messages across rather than rally support for ethnic identification and ethnic division (2000, pp.161-162). A similar case is found in the case of Taiwan's briefly important New Party, whose members were largely Mainlanders or sympathetic to reunification with China, but who nevertheless conducted some of their call-in programs in Tai-yu (ibid, p.162). The issue of which language to use and when in order to either mend or break an ethnic boundary line thus required much linguistic as well as political skill, as candidates soon discovered.

Chen Shui-bian and His Socio-political Predicaments[4]

Chen Shui-bian won the presidential election on March 18, 2000, with 39.3 percent of the vote, a number large enough to remove the KMT from the political limelight, yet too narrow to leave Chen with a mandate. As a "minority president" (*shaoshu zongtong*), Chen and his cabinet had to form a coalition government expected to tackle many difficult tasks, both on the domestic and international fronts. DPP hard-liners voiced increasingly nationalistic sentiments, with which Chen had to strike a balance in order to retain both presidential neutrality and partisan affiliation.

Chen also had to prove that he could work with the KMT mainstream, many of whom were upset at their election losses but still a majority in the Legislative Yuan and a force in many island-wide business sectors. Above all, Chen had to prove to China, and to the rest of the world, that he could handle all the domestic issues, maintain national dignity and prosperity, and negotiate with the PRC on terms and time frames acceptable to both sides.

These were no easy tasks for Chen, and he needed not only political skills but also linguistic skills to ease frictions and please foes. He was good at inspiring enthusiasm, especially among blue-collar workers and the younger generation with whom he could cement instant bonds by using indirect speech features such as analogy, allusion, and metaphor, performing these tasks in Tai-yu. Unlike most heavyweight politicians in Taiwan—the KMT's Ma Ying-jeou for example—who tended to emphasize their foreign education and training (especially in America) and impress the media and voters with their fluency in foreign languages (especially English), Chen inspired with his can-do spirit, maverick style, and pride in his humble background as a tenant farmer's son who fought his way up, first through poverty, then by earning a law degree at National Taiwan University, and finally by establishing himself gradually as a new political superstar in the then opposition party, the DPP.

He was praised as a straight A student who always out-studied and out-performed the rest of the class, yet he was criticized by one of his former advisers, Hsu Chung-hsin, as being a "100 percent lawyer." He was good at campaigning and was seen as one of the most popular politicians, especially among younger generations who not only loved the rock concerts the DPP threw during election campaigns but also snapped up the "A-Bian Family" doll, depicting Chen as cute, diminutive and marketable. Yet he also became tagged with arrogance, ruthlessly mowing down opponents, making enemies, and alienating friends (Cheng, 2000). A country boy and a tough politician, Chen's humble background, deep roots with his southern origins, and zest to climb to the top of the social ladder made some observers compare him with various determined American politicians. *Time* columnist Meg Greenfield remarked that 'he's a Taiwanese Al Gore, and that's part of his problem. He could do with a bit of Clintonian warmth and charm" (*Time* May 21, 2001). Like Gore, Chen was smart and slick at campaigning but had problems connecting with those whose emotions and hearts were set on critical issues such as, in Taiwan's case, cross-Strait ties, and party realignment.

In addition to winning, Chen also showed he could survive defeat and bounce back. He was jailed in 1986 for libel, yet was elected as Taipei mayor in 1994, in the first direct election for that post. He narrowly lost reelection as Taipei mayor in 1998 but then entered the 2000 presidential race and won. On the day of his defeat to Ma Ying-jeou for a second term as Taipei mayor, Chen cited a statement of Churchill, "A great city is known for the people's cruelty to their leader." Like Churchill, who later made a comeback after defeat in a local election, Chen was already preparing for his run for the presidency and finally won it in the 2000 race, the first time in Chinese history that an opposition party won the presidency. Chen's slim 39 percent of the vote was large enough to end the KMT's more than half a century administration, yet short of the mandate needed to combat the power of the Legislative Yuan dominated by the KMT majority. Many were dismissive of Chen and saw the outcome as the mere aftermath of a split between the pro-unification group in the KMT backing the official party candidate Lien Chan (23.1 percent of the vote) and the independent candidate James Soong (36.8 percent). In 2004, Chen ran for a second presidential term and won re-election again with 50.11 percent, a margin of only 0.22 percent over a combined Lien Chan-James Soong opposition ticket total of 49.89 percent. Lien from the KMT and Soong from the People First Party (PFP) refused to concede and challenged the results, though unsuccessfully.

Chen's ability to play to the media, to work with the crowd, to seize the moment and to relate to people from the working class was further evidenced in his autobiography, *Son of Taiwan*. Chen was also one of the many Taiwanese politicians willing to take on more than one role to get the job done, at least in costumes, during his campaigns. He dressed, notably, as Superman, a famous baseball player, and a male impersonator of the Statue of Liberty. He quoted the Bible and ancient Chinese texts and referred to himself as Joshua while anticipating a peaceful transition of power from the KMT to the DPP. Inspired by other politicians whose daring Chen took serious note of, he also compared himself to Nixon and South Korea's Kim Tae Chung in his handling of cross-Strait issues. Chen's rhetorical strategies further included switching from one dialect to another, for example, from Mandarin to Tai-yu, or by making reference to trendy achievers in movies and sports, such as movie stars in *Titanic* and *Superman*, and baseball favorites, or by using indirect speech such as allusion, analogy, and metaphor.

In sum, Chen was a seasoned politician who not only had the political skills but also the linguistic skills to deliver messages, to work the crowd, and to seize the moment. Studying his rhetorical strategies is a worthwhile exercise in understanding how language and politics work together in Taiwan's increasingly democratized society.

Texts and Discussion

In this section, we examine instances of Chen's switching between Mandarin and Tai-yu in the 2001 election. We first categorize the instances according to pragmatic functions such as emphasis, repetition, ease of communication, and message qualification. As we will see from the examples, most of the instances are in accordance with the principle of situational switching proposed by Gumperz (1982), which stresses that speakers modify their choice of codes according to macro social factors such as topic, participants, and settings. In addition, we also want to use these examples to suggest that an instance of codeswitching can have multiple readings, which can derive from the symbolic meanings of a chosen code, such as "we-code," or "they-code," and shared understandings and expectations among the interlocutors. Furthermore, such strategic ambiguities can serve the purposes of either boundary leveling or boundary-maintaining in a highly contested context such as an election campaign. The polyphony of codeswitching can be best explained by a Rational Choice (RC) model (Myers-Scotton and Bolonyai 2001) and can serve political purposes of inclusion or separation, when judged either from an intragroup or inter-group perspective. At the same time, a skilled politician can make his linguistic choice and calculation appealing to the public when codeswitching is performed in the company of puns, slang, or set phrases (*chengyu*).

Examples:[5]

6.1 chhiaN3-lang5 ui5 chiah, lan2 bo5 jim7-ho5 phian-kian3 kah seng5-kian3. kiat-koe2 li2 chit-ma2 iau3-lai5 **nng2 thou5 chhim kut8**, iau3-lai5. **de cun jin chi.**

Trans: "We do not have any prejudice in employing any officials. However, now they are going to bully me, to 'get an inch but demand a yard.'"

kong2 kin-a2-jit8 iong7 ah0 chit8 ko3 kok-bin5-tong2-chek tek lang5, iau3-lai5 cho3 heng5-cheng3-iN7-tiuN2, chiap-e7-lai5 i hi le tong2, **kui8 oaN2 iau3 phong2 koe3-khi3**, hit si7 put-kho2-leng5 e5 tai7-chi3. me chiong-kiat hek kim, ruguo **huan tang buhuan iao,** na2-tioh8-ai3 soan2 leh. (The example is taken from a SetN TV News item recorded on 03/31/89.)

Trans: Saying they [the ruling party] use a person with a KMT background to be the prime minister, and now they want to take over completely. This is impossible. To terminate the corruption . . . if you only change the solution without changing the prescription, then why do we need an election?

In the first example, Chen was talking to labor representatives and discussing his ideas of cooperation across party lines. At the same time, he was also accusing the opposition party, i.e. the KMT, of being too harsh and aggressive over his decisions regarding cabinet selections. In this example, we see three instances of changes of code, the first occurring right after Chen uses Taiwanese slang, **nng2 thou5 chhim kut8** (plowing deep in soft soil), which can be translated as "giving an inch, but demanding a yard." Chen further emphasizes this point by switching to Mandarin and using a literal phrase, **de cun jin chi**, which has a similar meaning to its Tai-yu counterpart. By making his point twice in both Tai-yu and Mandarin and in slang and set phrases, respectively, Chen is most likely trying to emphasize criticism of the KMT. Chen later uses indirect quotation and another Tai-yu slang expression, **kui8 oaN2 iau3 phong2 koe3-khi3** (taking over the entire bowl), to hint at the KMT's suspicion of an intent by Chen to replace the entire cabinet with his allies. What is interesting is that Chen not only uses indirect quotation to point out criticism of the opposition, but responds to such criticism by first pointing out the KMT's Achilles' heel—black gold, i.e. corruption and organized crime—then switching to a literal phrase in Mandarin, **huan tang bu huan iao**, (changing the solution without changing the prescription) and ending with a rhetorical question in Tai-yu to qualify his message. His later switch to the Mandarin literal phrase can have two interpretations: first, it is difficult to find an equivalent in Tai-yu, and second, we think that the use of the Mandarin literal phrase has a metaphorical meaning since here the topic, the participants, and the setting remain the same but Chen switches to Mandarin, a code that symbolizes officialdom and authority, to express his determination.

6.2 ruhe lai chaoyue dangpai qijian, ningju chaoye gongshi, jiangshi jueding shizheng chengbai de guanjian. chhut-kok piaN3 goa7-kau, teng5-lai5 beh piaN3 keN-che3. goa2 siong-sin3 put chi2-si7 teng5-lai5 piaN3 keN-che3, ma7 mel piaN3 ni5-be2. a piN2 ah choat8-tui3 e5-kah tak8-ke che2-iouN7 hap8-lit8 it-khi2, ia7 choat8-tui3 choan5-sim choan5-lit8 hou7 i theN-e7-khi3. (Speech made on 06/05/90. SetN News. Chen was lunching with DPP legislators, expressing his concerns and determination to improve the economy and win the December election.)

Trans: How to overcome partisan ideology, soliciting a consensus between the ruling party (DPP) and the opposition parties, will be a key point in the success of the government's performance. (I) go abroad in the cause of foreign affairs; (I) come back to strive for a better economy. I believe that I came back not only to strive for the economy but also for the end-of-the-year (election). A-bian will definitely work together with everybody and will hang on whole-heartedly for sure.

In the second example, Chen first stated his pressing agenda in Mandarin, i.e. overcoming partisan ideology and soliciting a consensus between the ruling party and the opposition parties. His choice of Mandarin can be explained by the nature of the statement, which is authoritative, official, and should be understood by people with or without any political affiliation. Mandarin as the national language certainly helps him achieve the above functions. Later, when he stresses his ambition and determination to improve the economic situation and to win the end-of-the-year election, he switches to Tai-yu, which functions as the "we-code" among the DPP members. His choice further helps solidify morale and gain access for himself to group membership.

6.3 a piN2 ah, kam2-sia7 lan2 tak8-ke e5 phah-piaN3, ia7 kam2-sia7 lan2 kok-ui7 e paN2 piaN3. chong2-si7, **zongyou yitian dengdao ni.** teng2 chap8 ji7 tang tan2-kau3, piau2-si7 siaN-pi? piau2-si7 lan2 chi2-iau3 u7 li2-siong2, lan2 u7 bok8-phiau, poe7 hong3-ki7, chhiu2-ho2 lan2 it-teng7 e7-hiau2 seng5-kong, tio3-m- tio3? (The example is taken from Chen's 11/04/01 campaign speech at Changhua, TVBS News. Chen thanked the audience for their patience and hard work and pointed out the twelve year wait for gaining entry into the World Trade Organization.)

Trans: A-bian appreciates everybody's efforts. I also thank you all for your hard work. After all, "(We will) finally reach you one day." We have waited for twelve years. What does this mean? This means that as long as we have an ideal or a goal, and we never give up, we will succeed in the long run. Right?

Here, Chen's switch to Mandarin is designed to introduce a quotation, which is the title of a popular song and has been used by many others on various occasions. To say it in Mandarin not only lends authenticity but also attracts attention. Further, Chen emphasizes the long wait for WTO by uttering a paraphrase in Tai-yu in the following sentence, and he ends with a rhetorical question, "What does this mean?" We think his switch between Mandarin and Tai-yu in this instance suggests the pragmatic functions of lending authenticity, making a quotation, getting attention, and stressing important issues.

6.4 kok-bin5-tong2 tioh8-si7 chit-ma2 kok-hoe7 e5 te7 it toa7 tong2, chai7-ia2-tong2 ka-khi2-lai5 saN-hun-chi-ji7 e5 sek8-chhu3, chit-ma2 iu7 te7 kong, iu7-koh ka7 i koe3-poaN3-sou2, lan2 cha2 chiu7 ka7 i koe3-poaN3-sou2 ah, kiat-koe2, you zenmeyang? chiong lan2 e5 i7-soan3 sat-tiau7, che2 si7 tui3 lan2 PheN5-ou5 lang5, tui3 lan2 li5-to2, choe3 toa7 e bu2-jiok8. (Chen gave this speech on 11/05/01 at Peng-Hu Island (Era News), where he criticized the opposition party legislators' boycotting of the budgets in the legislature.)

Trans: The KMT has the working majority in the legislature. The opposition parties make up two-thirds of it. Now (they) are saying that (we should) allow them more than half the seats. We let them have more than half the seats long ago. And, so what? (They) cut our budget. This is the greatest insult to us Peng-Hu people, to us off-island people.

In this example, Chen used Tai-yu in most junctures with the exception of "So what?" where he switched to Mandarin and dropped both of his hands when saying it. There are several interesting points in this instance: first, Chen's choice of Tai-yu is seen as accommodating the audience. His attempt to gain membership with the audience is further evidenced in the last junctures of the example, where he uses the inclusive first person plural pronoun "us/we" (lan2), while implying that the people who are the working majority in the legislature sand who boycotted the budget are "they." Notice that in Chen's first usage of "we" (lan2), there can be more than one reading of "we." That is, "we" can mean the voters who gave the KMT its working legislative majority, who are not necessarily from Peng-Hu, or it can refer to the audience, which did elect local KMT legislators. Although there are ambiguities in who "we" are, the audience should be pretty clear about the implied "they"—the working majority in the Legislative Yuan.[6] Chen's switch to Mandarin can be interpreted as attention getting, since he did so just after finishing a statement. Moreover, in viewing the videotape of this speech, we saw that he dropped both his hands while asking "So what?" in Mandarin, and this paralinguistic evidence informed us that Chen was also making an indirect negative comment by way of asking a semi-tag question in Mandarin. In his later utterance, the symbolic boundary we/they is concealed syntactically, since in Chinese, at least in conversation, it is not required that the subject position be filled, so long as the interlocutors can identify the agent from the context. Thus, Chen not only chose Tai-yu to identify with the audience but also simultaneously drew a symbolic boundary between "we" (Chen/the people at Peng-Hu) and "they" (the legislators who boycotted the budgets). In sum, the analyses of this example inform us that a switch of code can signal the speaker's intention to redefine boundaries, to gain membership, to get attention, and to make indirect negative comments.

6.5 a piN2 ah, u7 ki-hoe7 cho3 Tai5-pak-chhi7 chhi7-tiuN2, chai7 Tai5-pak a piN2 ah ia7 seng5-lip8 ji7-ji7-poeh ki3-liam7-koan2, ji7-ji7-poeh ho5-peng5 kong-hng5, put-chi2 chiam-tui3 ji7-ji7-poeh, chiam-tui3 koe3-khi3 peh8-sek e5 khiong2-pou3, a piN2 ah ma7 seng5-lip8 peh8-sek-khiong2-pou3 ki3-liam7-pi,lan2 hi-bong7 kong2,[7] muqin buzai kuqi, muqin zai wanshang buzai kuqi, meiyou zuqun zhifen, meiyou shengji zhibie, meiyou chaoye de butong. women ai zheyikuai tudi, women ai Taiwan, women buyao you zhengfu puohai, women buyao you renhe de baise kongbu, dui budui? (Chen made this speech at Jia-yi on 11/08/01, Era News. In this speech he mentioned that he had authorized the establishment of the 2/28 Memorial Museum, the 2/28 Peace Park, and the White Terror Memorial while serving as Taipei Mayor from 1994 to 1998. He later stressed his goals of transcending ethnic boundaries, avoiding clashes between the ruling party and the opposition parties, and putting an end to government persecutions.)

Trans: A-bian had the chance to be the mayor of Taipei. A-bian (helped) establish the museum memorializing the 2/28 Incident[8] and the 2/28 Peace Park.[9] These were done not only because of the 2/28 Incident, but also to remember the White Terror[10] in the past. A-bian also (helped) put up a monument to remember the White Terror.[11] We hope that mothers will cry no more, mothers cry no more at night. (There will be) no division among ethnic groups, no division between mainlanders and Taiwanese, and no division between the ruling party and the opposition parties. We love this land. We love Taiwan. We want no more persecution by the government. We want no more white terrors. Right?

Here, Chen starts his speech by letting the audience at Jia-yi know that he had contributed to and endorsed the democratization process during his tenure as Taipei mayor. His choice of Tai-yu can be seen as a symbolic convergence with the audience, and we further interpret this act of identity as his bid to gain approval from the audience. As we mentioned, before, democratization in Taiwan occurred in unison with the relaxing of language policy and the rise of Tai-yu and other ethnic languages, such as Hakka and aboriginal languages. The then-opposition party, the DPP, had used Tai-yu while engaging in debates and arguments with members at the Legislative Yuan and had demanded compensation and rights at various protests and sit-ins. In this context, Tai-yu can be seen as "the language for democratizing movements." Thus, it is not surprising that Chen describes his efforts for Taiwan's democratization in Tai-yu, especially in places such as Jia-yi, where the first 2/28 Incident monument was established and where Tai-yu is the unmarked choice. Chen later switches to Mandarin when he starts listing his goals of transcending partisan ideologies, overcoming ethnic boundaries, and eliminating government persecution, as witnessed by the 2/28 Incident and evident during the enforcement of martial law (from 1949 to 1987). His choice of an unmarked code in this context can be interpreted as a bid to reach out to a broader audience, i.e. not only the audience at Jia-yi but also all people in Taiwan, regardless of ethnic background and partisan affiliation. By choosing Mandarin, still the national language and a symbol for ethnic integration at this point, he shows himself as trying to bridge ethnic boundaries.

6.6   chong2-si7 bi7-lai5 ji7 tang poaN3, a piN2 ah ke3-siok8 cho3 chong2-thong2, **rang a-bian buhaozuo, dajia jiu buhaoguo.** bi7-lai5 ui5-liau2 beh hou7 a piN2 ah ho2 cho3, tak8-ke ho2-ke3, chiu7 iau3 chi-chhi5 a piN2 ah, chi-chhi5 bin5-chu2-chin3-pou7-tong2, ho7 bin5-chu2-chin3-pou7-tong2 seng5-ui5 kok-hoe7 te7 it toa7 tong2, a-ne ho2-m-ho2?   (Chen at Jia-yi on 11/08/01, Era News.)

48   Chapter Three

Trans: After all, in the coming two and a half years, A-bian will continuously be the president. If you leave A-bian in difficulty, you all will live in difficulty. In order to make A-bian's work easier and to make your lives easier in the future, you must support A-bian, support the DPP, and make the DPP the No. 1 party in the legislature. All right?

In this example, Chen first chose the unmarked code to identify with the audience. He later chose the marked code, Mandarin, and used a slogan-like phrase with rhymes and parallel construction to make the point of his being besieged by the opposition parties. It is interesting to point out the paralinguistic information provided by the video clip of this speech. We hear two heavy drumbeats and a pause when Chen utters this phrase. Within this context, we think that Chen's switch to Mandarin not only serves to qualify his previous message—he has been the president and will be the president for the next two and a half years—but also to escalate the conflict between himself and the opposition parties. Furthermore, as in example 6.4, he is making an indirect threat, emphasizing what he has been through and the consequences for the people of the continuation of his besieged situation.

6.7 u7 chit8 tiau5 i7-soan3, ge5 siu-jip8 hou7 song3-hiong-lang5 e5 kiaN2-li5, heng3-kian3 thok-ji5-sou2 hou7 in kiaN2-li5, kai2-sian7 siat-pi7, phian-liat8 che7-chio2 nia7-nia7? neng-pek chap8-chhit ban7-it chheng goan5, a-ne ma7 sat? **gewei zaiye, zai zenmeye,** zenme neng shandiao women de jiaoyu yusuan ? zenme neng shandiao women de fuli yusuan, dui budui? (Chen at Jia-yi on 11/08/01, Era News.)

Trans: "There was a budget for the children of lower-income families to build child care centers and to improve facilities. How much did it provide for? 2,170,000 NT dollars. How could they cut it? Those people of the opposition parties [pronounced the same as "barbarous"], however barbarous you are, how could you cut our education budget? How could you cut our social welfare budget? Right?"

Here, the homonym "ye," which can mean either the opposition or barbarous, is employed and is further incorporated in Chen's choice of Mandarin. His switch to Mandarin might reflect his intention to get attention and escalate conflict between himself and the opposition parties, as further evidenced by the two interrogative sentences: "How can they cut the education budget?" and "How can they cut the welfare budget?" The two interrogative sentences can also signal his frustration at the budget cut and thus serve as indirect negative commentary. Last, Chen's use of a tag question at the end of this speech, serves both as a confirmation of his previous questions and to solicit attention and response from the audience.

6.8 cheng3-tong2 lun5-the3 chi-au7, che si7 te7 it pai2 choan5-kok-seng3 e5 tai7-soan2, women shi wanzhen de! (Chen made this campaign speech at Ilan on 11/09/01, Era News. He stressed the importance of the up-coming election.)

Trans: Since the alternation of the political parties, this is the first national election campaign we have had. We are very serious.

In this example, Chen taps into the official authority of Mandarin and uses it to qualify the message and to express his seriousness. His switch to Mandarin at the end of the sentence can also be interpreted as an attempt to get the audience's attention.

6.9 ui7-sim7-mih a piN2 ah phaiN choe3? chit8 ni5 goa7 lai5 tioh8-si7 **chu-xin-ji-lu,** yaoba a-bian laxialai, bu chengren a-bian shi zongtong, mei banfa jieshou a-bian shi dajia xuanchu lai de zongtong, bun7-te5 chiu7 chhut te7 chia, bu8 un7-tong7-ka e5 cheng-sin5, bu8 bin5-chu2 e hong-hoan7, sou2-i2 lin2 bat bun7-te5 e5 koan-kian7 te-da2. (Chen made this campaign speech at Yun-lin 11/12/01. He complained that the opposition parties had been boycotting him, refusing to accept the reality that Chen had been elected president. Era News.)

Trans: Why has A-bian worked with difficulty? For more than one year, they have been seeking every opportunity to pull A-bian down. They don't acknowledge A-bian is president. They can't accept that A-bian is the president you all elected. This is the problem: they have no sportsmanship; they have no democratic style. So you know what the key point of the problem is.

Chen started his speech in this example with the unmarked language, Tai-yu, since Yun-lin, a city in southern Taiwan, has a large population of Tai-yu speaking voters. His later switch to Mandarin is triggered by a Mandarin set phrase, **"chu-xin-ji-lu,"** which can be roughly translated as "working very hard," or "seeking every opportunity." There is no Tai-yu equivalent to this phrase, and Chen's switch to Mandarin at this juncture can be explained as using a Mandarin phrase to support his point. But Chen doesn't stop at this phrase. He goes on in Mandarin to criticize the opposition parties for not acknowledging Chen as the president and to condemn them for not accepting Chen as a duly elected president. In this context, his use of Mandarin serves to escalate the conflict between himself and the opposition parties.

6.10 khioh2 pun-soe2 khioh-tioh8 Tai5-pak-koan7, lan2 u7-kau3 chheng-khi3, m7-thang chai3 khioh2 pun-soe2, tio3-m-tio3? lan2 si7 te7 soan2 chhi7-tiuN2, m7-si7 te3 ho lang5 zuo fanlanjun de zuhe, m7-si7 beh choe3-lang5 e5 bailaoshu, cho3 chit8 ko3 cheng3-tong2 kiat-hap8 tek sit8-giam7-tiouN5. a piN2 ah pai3-thok toa7-ka, women jujue zuo *bailaoshu,* gun2 beh soan2 ho2 koan7-tiuN2 sou-cheng-chhiong, tio3-m-tio3? (Chen's campaign speech was made on 11/16/01 in Taipei County. Chen was trying to lobby votes for the incumbent county chief Su Zhen-chang while criticizing Su's close opponent, Wang Chien-shiuan, a New Party nominee, who was also winning support from the KMT and the People's First Party. Era News.)

Trans: He (Wang Chien-shiuan) came to Taipei County to pick up trash.[12] We are very clean and we don't need trash to be picked up, right? We are voting for a mayor, not to give a chance to the organization of the pan-blue[13] alliances, not to be a guinea pig for others, not to be a laboratory for hodgepodge political alliances. A-bian asks you all to refuse to be guinea pigs. We will vote for the good county chief Su Zhen-chang.

Here, Chen switches to Mandarin three times in his campaign speech. In Taipei County, the default language is Tai-yu. The first switch saw a new political coinage, *fanlanjun de zuhe* (pan-blue alliance), which referred to the cooperation among the KMT, the New Party (NP), and the People First Party (PFP). Chen was backing the DPP incumbent, Su Zhen-chang, and criticizing Su's tough challenger, Wang Chien-shiuan, the NP candidate who had also won endorsement from the KMT and the PFP. The fact that Wang got an endorsement and support from the opposition parties threatened Su, since polls showed that Wang and Su remained close, within 2 percent of each other. Chen's initial switch to Mandarin can be explained by the lack of a proper equivalent in Tai-yu. Second, Chen switches to Mandarin for a similar reason when he refers to the *fanlanjun de zuhe* (pan-blue alliance) as an experiment of hodgepodge political alliances, and urges the audience not to be a guinea pig or take part in it. Lastly, Chen switches to Mandarin again in order to reiterate his point of not taking part in the pan-blue hodgepodge alliance, repeating that "we refuse to be guinea pigs." Thus, his last switch to Mandarin can be explained by the lack of an equivalent in Tai-yu and as a reiteration of the previous point.

6.11 kok-ui7, kok-ui7, iau2-u7 it ui7, iau2-u7 chit8-ui7 chai7 po3-choa2 tian7-si7 u7 khoaN3-tiu3, te7 kong2 siaN2-mih oe7, i kong2 wo meiyou luoxuan, qunian sanyue bahao wo meiyou luoxun, wo shi bei zuodiao de, li2 beh thiaN kui2 pian3? gewei, ta meiyou luoxuan ma? ta you meiyou luoxuan? ta you meiyou luoxuan? (Chen made this campaign speech at Jia-yi where he criticized James Soong, the 2000 presidential candidate and the chairperson of the PFP, for blaming his defeat on being "framed." 10/27/01 Era News.)

Trans: Everybody, everybody, there is another one, another one who you have either read of in newspapers or seen on TV. What did he say? He said: "I didn't loose. On March 8 of last year, I didn't loose. I was framed." How many times do we have to listen to this? Everybody, didn't he lose? Did he lose? Did he lose?

In this example, Chen uses the unmarked language, Tai-yu, and the marked language, Mandarin, interchangeably. He starts the speech in Tai-yu, asking the audience if they are aware of one of the presidential candidates in the 2000 election, James Soong, claimed that he (Soong) didn't lose; instead, he had been framed (by the KMT). Chen quotes Soong's speech in Mandarin and this has at least three stylistic effects: 1) the quote of Soong's speech gains authenticity, since Soong had been considered a *waishengren*, or Mainlander, whose used Mandarin in most situations; 2) variation and contrast is offered in the speech so that Chen can attract the audience's attention; 3) a confrontation is escalated and Chen's dismay at Soong's statement is expressed, as further evidenced from paralinguistic information in the video clip, where Chen can be seen dropping both of this hands when making this utterance. Moreover, Chen's distress is evidenced from the next two sentences where he repetitively asks, "Didn't he lose (the presidential election)?" twice in Mandarin, while pointing at the audience and soliciting positive answers. The confrontation finally reaches its peak when Chen repeats the last question again to the audience and we hear the audience saying, "Yes!" on the video clip.

Summary and Conclusions

In this chapter, we have tried to extend the study of codeswitching to an often-neglected discourse—political campaigns. By using Chen Shui-bian's campaign speeches in the 2001 election as a source, we have demonstrated that besides achieving pragmatic functions, codeswitching in political discourse can also serve as a disclaimer of performance, further helping the speaker to avoid responsibility, escalate confrontation or slip into other roles. These symbolic acts of identity can be achieved because of the indeterminacy of codeswitching. In addition, by adopting the Rational Choice model, we have demonstrated how the model helps a politician make rational choices from an array of languages in order to maximize benefits and minimize risks. We have provided evidence that, in this case, Tai-yu—the vernacular language, the language spoken by the majority population in Taiwan, especially in southern Taiwan, and the language long used by the then opposition party, the DPP—is used by Chen not only to create socio-pragmatic discoursal effects, but also for boundary marking (ex. 6.1, 6.2), and for taking refuge in, in order to disclaim performance and escape responsibility and obligations as well (ex. 6.10). Chen uses Mandarin, the official language, the language chosen by the KMT for administration, education, and other public domains, and the lingua franca for people in Taiwan when there is a lack of equivalence (ex. 6.1) in Tai-yu, when he wants to attract attention and lend authority (ex. 6.3, 6.6, 6.8), or when he tries to escalate conflicts or make indirect negative comments (ex. 6.4, 6.7, 6.9, 6.11) and when he tries to level ethnic boundaries (ex. 6.5).

Implications

Our data and analyses have indicated that Chen's choice and use of Tai-yu in public domains is in accordance with the changing socio-political position between Tai-yu and Mandarin. As the DPP became the ruling party after its victory in the 2000 presidential election, the president, as well as other officials and politicians, used Tai-yu in public speeches and for official functions. Moreover, in light of the heightened consciousness of rights shown by interest groups, language choice and alternation between Mandarin and other Chinese varieties took on acute political connotations. Such linguistic practices not only helped elevate the status of Chinese varieties other than Mandarin but also challenged the status of Mandarin. Although exactly what the official language(s) in Taiwan should be is still the subject of heated debate, we have already seen a much more relaxed language policy and integrated attitude toward vernacular languages.

In Chapter 4, we will continue our focus on language choices in political oratory, using the oratory of aspiring presidential candidates to illustrate that, given the conflicting socio-political ideologies associated with Mandarin and Tai-yu, a choice between Mandarin and Tai-yu is equivalent to a duel between historical determinism and political pragmatism.

Notes

1. According to Ian Buruma, an East Asia specialist who has published widely on political development in Taiwan, the most powerful driving force propelling Taiwan's newborn democracy is not a rising standard of living but a peculiar kind of nationalism, which pits those Chinese whose ancestors came to Taiwan over the past several centuries, that is ethnic Taiwanese, against those who fled to Taiwan from the mainland in 1949, that is Mainlanders (Buruma 1997, pp. 78-90).

2. This is the Hanyu Pinyin spelling of the Wade-Giles Romanization, Kuomintang (KMT).

3. It was estimated that by the end of the Second World War, 40 percent of the population could speak Japanese and 70 percent of the school children were literate in Japanese (Hsiau 1997).

4. The following section is revised from Wei (2001b).

5. For the data analysis and transcriptions, utterances in Tai-yu are underlined while those in Mandarin are not. Mandarin examples are transcribed in Pinyin and Tai-yu is transcribed in Church Romanization. The author also adopts the Mandarin/Tai-yu Translation System provided by Professor Chen Xing-xi at the Department of Information Science of National Taiwan University to transcribe the Tai-yu examples. Special use of homonyms, puns, slang and *chengyu* are in boldface.

6. In the 2001 election, the DPP won the most seats of any party in the Legislative Yuan, but did not win an absolute majority. The KMT lost its absolute legislative majority and its mandate in the race.

7. Chen was quoting a sentence inscribed on the White Terror Memorial on Green Island, where the original can be translated: "In that era, many mothers spent nights crying for their children locked up on Green Island."

8. The Incident referred to was a violent one, beginning in Taipei on February 28, 1947 after personnel of the Taiwan Tobaccos and Wines Monopoly Bureau beat a female vendor for illegally peddling cigarettes and accidentally killed a bystander. Crowds attacked the bureau's offices, and the resulting crackdown provoked island-wide riots and repression that caused heavy causalities. The violence gradually subsided after Taiwan governor Chen Yi launched a "clean-up" action on March 20 of that year (*Central Agency News*, 02/26/01).

9. The 2/28 Peace Park (*er-er-ba heping gongyuan*) was established in 1995. Ex-president Lee Teng-hui made a public apology at the opening ceremony to the victims of the 2/28 Incident (see footnote 7 for background information) and to their families. In the same year, the legislature approved compensation for families of the victims of 2/28. The Administrative Yuan established a foundation to solicit funds and support.

10. "White Terror" refers to the tight control by the KMT over Taiwan starting in the late 1940s. It was instituted with statutes dating from 1949-50 when the ROC declared martial law and enacted "Measures to Eradicate Espionage during the Period of Communist Rebellion," and ended with the repeal of martial law in 1987. During this period, many were jailed after being falsely accused of crimes or practicing civil disobedience (*Sinoroma*, 07/1997, Taipei, Taiwan).

11. Completed in 2000 on Green Island, where many of the victims of the White Terror were jailed, the monument is a special memorial to the victims and aims to transcend sadness and the sense of tragedy. It is also the site of Asia's first monument to human rights (ibid).

12. Wang emphasized that he wanted to run a "clean" election, i.e. his campaign would not litter the streets with flags, slogans, or banners, a practice most other candidates take for granted.

13. Blue referred to the KMT, yellow to the New Party, and orange to the People's First Party. All three opposition parties tried to form alliances in order to win the election, hence the "pan" colors.

Chapter 4
Language Choice and Politics

In this chapter, we argue that a choice of Mandarin or Tai-yu for the aspiring Taiwan politician correlates with the politician's vision of Taiwan's status as a vulnerable nation/state. Our argument is made by conceptualizing the meaning of using a language in contingent socio-historical moments and by contextualizing the choice of a language as political struggle for legitimacy and resources. Taiwan's colonial past, the rights and representation demanded by competing interest groups, and the island's stability and prosperity in relation to China provide grounds for debate and imagination concerning a national identity. Conflicting ideologies vis-à-vis all things Chinese and Taiwanese—the former ideology premised on cultural-historical determinacy, the latter on political pragmatism—take center stage in a Taiwan election platform. The questions we ask are, first, how do the politics of difference, made complicated by competing nationalist visions and by a mixture of economic-political pragmatism regarding different administrations, play into the notion of "becoming Taiwanese"? Second, what are the linguistic strategies adopted by aspiring politicians to articulate and negotiate dialogical imagination with regard to forces of cultural identification and to political alternatives? Simple questions such as "Who are we?" and "Where do we want to go?" asked in Mandarin or in Tai-yu can strike emotional chords and make or break the results of an important race, even a presidential election.

The 1995 televised presidential campaign speeches by DPP candidates provide an invaluable source for our approach, not only because the 1996 presidential election was the first direct presidential election in Chinese history but also because the then opposition party, the DPP, was widely seen as coming of age to contend with the KMT on issues of national identity and Taiwan's political future. We adopt the notion of Hall (1996) that identities are "constructed within, not outside, discourse. We need to understand them as produced in specific historical and institutional sites within specific discursive formations and practices by specifically enunciative strategies" (1996, p. 4). Moreover, identities emerge within the play of specific modalities of power, and thus are more the product of the marking of difference and exclusion than a sign of an identical, naturally constituted unity (ibid). Similarly, Ching (2001) argues that Japanese and Japaneseness, Taiwanese and Taiwaneseness, aborigines and aboriginality, and Chinese and Chineseness—as embodied in compartmentalized national, racial, or cultural categories—do not exist outside the temporality and spatiality of colonial modernity but are instead enabled by it (2001, p. 11). Ching further suggests, "We need to examine the processes and the procedures by which those categories [imagined communities and identities] are produced by colonial modernity, and how they are mobilized in turn as a regime of colonial power" (ibid, p. 5). The question we ask regarding the politics of identity and language choice is this: how have historical differences and identities presented and constructed in imperial China, colonial Japan and Nationalist (KMT) Taiwan provided inspirations and possibilities for an emerging Taiwanese identity? In our answer, we adopt Bakhtin's notions of "translinguistics" and "dialogues" to help us see language as an ideological site where different voices contest for domination. Under this framework, the analysis of language choice can be seen in terms of speakers trying to adopt either of opposed ideologies that admit the possibility for dominance (Bakhtin 1981; Hill and Hill 1986).

The chapter is structured into the following sections: 1) language choice historically from colonialism to emerging democracy; 2) the changing meaning of becoming Taiwanese; 3) language choice in a socio-political context; 4) ambiguities in language choice; 5) texts and discussions; 6) conclusion; 7) implications.

Language Choice from Colonialism to Emerging Democracy

Twice in Taiwan's history, a non-indigenous language was chosen and used as the "national" language. The first time was during the Japanese occupation (1895-1945) when the imposition of Japanese upon Taiwan helped spread the ideology of pan-Japanism (*huang-min zhengce*) and facilitated the control and rule of the people of Taiwan. The second instance was after the KMT's defeat by the CCP on the Chinese mainland, an event causing large groups of soldiers, bureaucrats and others to flee to Taiwan in the late 1940s at a time when large-scale promotion of Mandarin by the Mandarin Promotion Committee (*Guoyu Tuixing Weiyuanhui*) and other governmental bodies and schools had already begun in the mainland.

The KMT regime replaced Japanese with Mandarin as the "national" language and mandated an exclusive language policy in which only Mandarin was to be taught at school and used at school and on official occasions.[1] Initially, during the early stages of the regime's takeover, other Chinese varieties, such as Hakka and Tai-yu, could still be used in public. The main objective at first was to rid Taiwan of all Japanese influence and to facilitate communication among people speaking different tongues. The policy took a more drastic term in the 1960s with the ban on the other Chinese varieties and aboriginal languages. Similar measures had also been taken by the previous Japanese administration under wartime conditions during the last stages of their rule.[2] The KMT's implementation of Mandarin as the "national" language (Guoyu) served social and political purposes in addition to ridding the people of previous Japanese influence. Speaking Guoyu was considered essential to converting the Taiwanese to become Chinese and as a pretext for the ultimate reunification of the motherland. There were obvious cultural, linguistic and political differences then, and none of these could have been resolved easily without altering the sentiments and expectations of the people. The importance of speaking correct Guoyu was synonymous with being Chinese, an objective planned and executed with the assistance of a state controlled media and an education system prepared to propagate and inculcate Chinese civilization and history. In addition, as Chun (2000) rightly points out, "The forced imposition of Mandarin as the standard medium for official purposes was an important precondition for propagation of Chinese nationalism and the mandate of a continuous history, all of which had as its intended goal the eradication and subordination of local ethnic languages and tradition to the political mainstream" (cf. ibid, p.13). As a result of such highhanded language policy, backed as it was by an imposition of stringent martial law, Chinese varieties such as Tai-yu, Hakka, and other local tongues, even those spoken by some KMT soldiers and officials as well as Malay-Polynesian aboriginal languages, were banned from public domains, and people were sometimes punished if they were heard using them.[3] Prevailing and all-encompassing nationalism and patriotism further dictated that speakers of non-Mandarin linguistic varieties be held in general suspicion by authorities.

The intrinsic link between language and identity makes the national language a coveted political symbol and an essential element of an assimilation policy. Speaking Japanese during the Japanese occupation period, or speaking Mandarin during the heyday of the KMT regime, not only was associated with a national identity ("being Japanese" or "being Chinese") but also with a high cultural identity tantamount in the contemporary establishment's terms to enlightenment and civilization.

The Japanese and KMT monolingual policies, accompanied by centralized education programs, helped assimilate the locals at the expense of indigenous cultural and linguistic practices. As integration became intense, both language and education policies were overbearing and created new classes among the people, stirring grievances. The imposition of a state language and the forbidding of mother tongues became an emotionally charged topic, especially among the creative set as popular entertainment and revolutionary ideas could be dismissed easily and denied any medium for propagation. For example, during the Japanese era, local theater groups such as the *budaixi* troupes (whose puppet shows featured wooden expressions and jerky movements, plots and customs inspired from ancient Chinese sources, and constantly presented martial arts effects) were asked to perform in Japanese with plots adjusted to extol the Japanese martial spirit. The replacement of the Japanese by the KMT in 1945 brought Standard Chinese to the performance of *budaixi*. In the 1960s, televised *budaixi* were banned for allegedly distracting islanders from their work.[4]

Not surprisingly, under the Japanese colonial regime, progressive ideas proved hard to propagate. The enlightened not only had to adapt to language discrepancies among the masses, speaking Japanese, Chinese and local varieties depending on the audience (the literate were mostly educated in Chinese and Japanese), but also had to consider limits placed on their freedoms and means by the administration. The early twentieth century should have been a prime time in Taiwan to test reform ideas. In addition to the progressive thinking flowing from the May Fourth Movement,[5] some of the brightest on the island had an extra advantage with coveted educations gained in Tokyo, but even these individuals faced limited tolerance by the Japanese administration. Some of the progressive ideas they tried, such as implementation of Chinese education, were immediately rejected as the authorities intensified their efforts to keep the island free from Chinese influence. Others such as the *baihuawen* movement in the 1920s and 1930s gained a limited acceptance, and still others such as the written Taiwanese (Tai-yu) movement created polarized ideas that still resonate today.[6] To illustrate with examples: Chang (2003) proposes that earlier, a collective Taiwanese consciousness flowered in the 1920s with young, aspiring Taiwanese frustrated with their fate under the Japanese colonization trying to emulate their Chinese counterparts on the mainland in the wake of the famous anti-imperialist, anti-Confucian May Fourth Movement (cf. pp. 23-24). Rigger (1999) states that Taiwan's movement for greater autonomy began in 1918. Taiwanese students living in Tokyo found inspiration in President Woodrow Wilson's worldwide campaign for national self-determination and human rights; they took further encouragement from Japanese rhetoric (addressed to Western governments) asserting the principle of racial equality. In 1921, a group of Taiwanese in Japan founded the Taiwan Culture Society. The group later split but some of the offshoots became the League for Local Self-Government (ibid, p. 35). These reform efforts were short-lived. Japanese policies in Taiwan promoting assimilation and mobilization for war and wartime production brushed aside tentative steps taken for home rule. Nevertheless, Taiwan's brief experience with elections set the tone for the future (ibid, p. 38). Heylen (2005) notes that throughout the 1920s and 1930s, the Taiwanese home-front mobilization movement organized lectures, summer schools and other activities to encourage the population at large to participate in the cultural advancement of Taiwanese society. These events were announced in vernacular journals, and were conducted in spoken Taiwanese not just Japanese. The professional elite—doctors, dentists and lawyers—communicated with their patients in Taiwanese, even though written prescriptions and legal documents had to be in Japanese. Nationalist-minded intellectuals convened and talked in Taiwanese, but presented their petitions and applications to the colonial authorities in Japanese. Personal writings either used Japanese, Classical Chinese and/or Mandarin Chinese (ibid, p. 504).

Illustrative of the Mandarin *baihuawen* movement was the vernacular newspaper *Taiwan Minpao* (1923-1936), published in Mandarin Chinese. This was tolerated by the authorities partly because an emerging Taiwanese middle class with purchasing power ran the newspaper, partly because advertisements were mainly in Japanese, and partly because the editors promised not to engage in political propaganda (ibid, p. 503). The use of Mandarin Chinese in various literary genres in the newspaper served several strategic ends. First, it was the language of the new era as proposed by the Chinese intellectuals on the mainland. Secondly, according to Heylen, it further served as defiance of the idea of the superiority of the Japanese script (ibid). Thirdly and ironically, the standardization of Mandarin Chinese on the mainland further inspired the subsequent written Taiwanese movement in the 1930s.

Chang (2003) mentions that the language hurdle among liberals and the masses alike, and the lack of a medium for spreading popular and progressive ideas, not only explains why the newly emerged Taiwanese identity failed to reach a large audience, but also helps us appreciate why Japanese education was so successful in nurturing Japanese patriotism and Japanese inclinations without serious challenge from the Taiwanese general public (ibid, p. 37). Ironically, on a similar line, a high-handed quintessential Chinese education policy installed by the KMT, coupled with tough laws to monitor irregular behavior, also proved to be efficient in silencing dissent and facilitating the implementation of economic and social development programs. Nevertheless, the seeds of resentment find their ways to germinate. As happened in Taiwan, eventually they branch out, reaching for a higher sky and bearing fruits extraordinary.[7]

Apart from the stringent national policies brought by both the Japanese and KMT administrations, considerable economic changes which subsequently contributed to socio-political changes and language changes also took place at this time. We think it desirable at this point to look into these "positive" economic developments and their consequent effects in encouraging the people of the island to develop a distinct sense of self and to search for language choices more politically ideal, i.e. those that might set off the Taiwanese first from the Japanese in the 1920s, then from the KMT Chinese after 1945, and lastly from the Chinese on the mainland since the 1980s, if not also from the supra-ethnic Chinese of the twenty-first century or indeed as part of that movement.

Under Japanese control from 1895 to 1945, Taiwan's economy prospered with increasing agricultural productivity, improved economic infrastructure, hydroelectric generation, and improved public hygiene, all of which elevated Taiwan's economic performance to a position second only to Japan's in Asia. The Qing Dynasty's attention to Taiwan before 1895 had been too little and too late and certainly could not compare with Tokyo's determination to make its first colony a showcase argument for Japanese imperial leadership in Asia. In the 1950s, the KMT, which had done poorly with its economic policies on the mainland, tried with well targeted U.S. financial assistance to improve the island's conditions. Some even argued that the combination of a failed experience, an estrangement with Taiwan's elite cemented by events such as the 2/28 Incident, and the administration's self-consciousness of its popular image as an "outside" regime, together with U.S. support and the existing Japanese economic infrastructure, gave the KMT significant leverage to make good plans and execute them well. According to Rigger (1999), the KMT didn't have to bend to the will of local capitalists and social luminaries, a sharp contrast from their dealings with the resistance of the wealthy Chinese on the mainland. Moreover, the 2/28 Incident proved that elites were as vulnerable to repression as any group and made them extremely reluctant to challenge the regime. As a result, some of the more liberal policies that the KMT had considered but abandoned on the mainland became cornerstones of Taiwan's economic development from 1950 on (cf. pp. 67-68).

Among the most successful policies were land reform[8] (1949-1953), followed by industrial development managed by a group of technocrats, mostly western-educated engineers and economists who enjoyed trust and autonomy from the administration and who designed and implemented a highly successful industrial policy based first on import substitution and then on export-oriented industrialization (cf. ibid, pp. 68-69). Similarly, Copper (1996) provides the following explanation for Taiwan's warp speed industrial development. The elements were: (1) the expansion of industrial employment; (2) increases in labor productivity; (3) U.S. economic assistance; (4) privatization; (5) a high rate of local savings and foreign investment; (6) a solid economic infrastructure, including transportation and efficient port facilities; and (7) excellent planning both by the government and the business community (p. 121). During this time, as mentioned, the U.S. was providing Taiwan with economic and military aid, which extended well into the 1960s. It was encouraging productive investment and offering expert advice. In fact, from the early 1950s to about 1960, U.S. aid provided 40 percent of Taiwan's capital formation, most of it helping the industrial sector. Few underdeveloped nations at that time or since have benefited as much in terms of economic growth generated by foreign aid (ibid, p. 122).

The harsh socio-political climate and ongoing tension between the administration and the society ironically proved to be a boon for the island's economy, for it smoothed the path for land reform and eased the autonomy enjoyed by the technocrats, whose autonomous monopoly of power was enjoyed by few other social elites until the situation started to change in the 1980s. In fact, in the 1960s and 1970s, what was most visible to observers in Taiwan and internationally was the blossoming of the economy, not new seeds of resentment that some of the economic policies were sowing. Between 1960 and 1980, per capita GNP increased from US$130 to US$2,100. Taiwan's GNP growth rate from 1960 to 1982 averaged 8.4 percent per year. At the same time, income distribution remained relatively egalitarian (Rigger 1999, p. 70).

The political consequences of egalitarian economic prosperity coupled with a relaxation of administrative controls starting in the late 1980s—notably the lifting of martial law in 1987—brought great momentum in socio-political transformation. Language once again became an important issue in a period of political transition. Opposition political parties, legalized following the creation of the

DPP in 1986, were soon to end the KMT's four decade monopoly of power. Sixty-seven parties besides the KMT registered with the government as of the summer of 1992.[9] Which language was to be used to express a wide array of sentiments—frustrations with language and political monopoly, for example, disquiet over ethno-linguistic injustices, as well as uncertainty toward the future of Taiwan's fate vis-à-vis China—once again became a heated matter.

C. F. Shih (2002) explores the interplay between language policy and ethnic politics/identity in the context of Taiwan's "Native vs. Mainlander" competition. Linguistic differences are examined as one of the instruments forging group solidarity or maintaining structural inequalities, and five waves of a linguistic/cultural renaissance undertaken by natives since the 1970s are documented. Hobbling the surges were the daunting logistical tasks and the questionable practicality of implementing "mother tongue" language education in elementary schools in the face of decreasing national budgets and a lack of teachers with the requisite proficiency and professional training (more discussion on a revised language policy appears in Chapter 5). In light of these factors, the linguistic revitalization of Chinese varieties and the aboriginal languages seemed more like reverse discrimination against Mandarin and part of the overall desinification (*qu Zhongguohua*) program of the DPP administration. Moreover, language policy seemed subsumed by a proxy war for power and legitimacy further complicated by the question of future relations with China and the pending identity quest of the Taiwan people.

In sum, in this section, we see that the choice and use of a certain language in Taiwan, at least at the national level starting with the Japanese colonization, has always been a political strategy to exert systematic pressure in order to ensure colonial/imperial control, to suppress as well as subordinate other linguistic and cultural practices, to consolidate ethnic consciousnesses, and to spread nationalism, patriotism or pluralism. Such political strategies regarding language use were further enforced and implemented through existing institutional means serving as the means to accomplish various ideological ends. With the KMT losing its political monopoly in Taiwan, the then opposition party, the DPP, chose Tai-yu as "the language for the people" to challenge the legitimacy and authority of Mandarin and its long held China-center social and political policies. In the midst of the fledgling party's quest for power, contending issues on the subject of correcting past wrongs and the quest for rights, including language rights for minorities as well as mother tongue language education (among other social issues) proved to be one of the DPP's winning cards in the quest for resources and representation. In the next section, we will examine how competing nationalistic visions, demands for democratization, and a newly developed pragmatism, combined with ambivalence over the new and increasing dependence on China's economy and suspicion of the PRC's engrossing nationalism, began changing the way Taiwan people saw themselves.

The Changing Meaning of Becoming Taiwanese

Chang (2003) argues that national identity arises, or emerges, for reasons that are much broader than sentiment and the need for belonging. In his view, such identity is always constituted with normative discourse, and is argued for and supported with forceful moral-political claims (2003, p. 23). Rather than linking national identity to a pre-existing locale or primordial sentiment, Chang argues for an ontological approach, opting to look into the various historical conditions giving rise to the evolution of the consciousness and meaning of a particular collective identity. He claims that the origin of the Taiwanese nationalistic idea can be traced back to at least the 1920s, but that the "maturation" of Taiwanese identity or the convergence of its many sources, did not take place until the late 1980s and is still not a fully-grown nationalism in the present day (ibid, p. 25). He also states that the convergence and development in Taiwan's case is not an inevitable consequence of ethno-conflicts or a matter of asymmetrical ethnic relations between Mainlanders and Taiwanese, although it is now so interpreted generally (ibid, p. 26).

On a similar note, Ching (2001) shows that Taiwanese identities were produced in the interstices of Qing colonial Taiwan, imperialist Japan and Nationalist (KMT) China. In addition, Ching offers a radical critique of colonial discourse that goes beyond merely pointing out the truisms that nations are "imagined communities" and identities are "historically contingent." The critique examines the processes and procedures by which those categories are produced by colonial modernity, and shows how they are mobilized in turn as regimes of colonial power (cf. Ching 2001, p. 5). Brown (2004) claims that identity is shaped by social experience, not culture or ancestry as is commonly claimed in political rhetoric. Our analyses support Chang and Ching's theses in recognizing socio-historical contingencies for the rise of a national consciousness and the importance of the colonial politics of nationalism and post colonial political identities. We take Brown's proposal a step further and point out the assimilationist mentality of the colonial administrations, Japanese and KMT alike. The mentality in each case featured a continuous civilization, shared ancestry and a common language. Directed at Taiwan, it not only aimed to erase internal differences among people, creating a unique cultural/linguistic/national identity with well-defined boundaries to exclude others, but also effectively changed the cultural and language landscape. Weller (2000) points out that the monolithic conviction implicit in a particular identity bears resemblance to the "blood and soil" rhetoric underlying Nazi German and Afrikaner constructions of identity. As in the reactions to the Nazi movement and apartheid, frustrations in Taiwan with a repressive regime and a single identity inspired many to consider identity pluralistically (more discussion on an alternative view of pluralistic identity will appear in Chapter 6). The colonial subjects' frustrations and inferiority complexes further created momentum for subsequent socio-political transformation, building demand for home-rule and autonomy.

The end of the Japanese rule in 1945 and the subsequent mass immigration of KMT personnel to Taiwan, in which close to two million persons from all parts of China arrived on Taiwan's shores eventually, brought new meanings to the idea of being Taiwanese. The term *benshengren*, i.e. those who arrived before 1945, in contrast to the term *waishengren*, those who came starting from 1945, depicts not only the status of Taiwan as a province or *sheng* of China (province or *sheng* was a term endorsed officially by the KMT in 1949), but also conveys a sense distinct social classes, language and cultural practices as well as clashing political views.

While some scholars stress the differences between the local and mainland groups, others go further to see the critical political consequence of the many conflicts and their effects on forging an ultimate Taiwanese national consciousness. For example, Wachman (1994b) states that whether the term "Taiwanese"[10] (*benshengren*) or "Mainlander" (*waishengren*) is used, the labels refer to Taiwan as a Chinese province rather than an independent state, placing more emphasis on one's ancestral place of origin than on one's place of birth. In terms of their political inclination and outlook, *benshengren* who were already in Taiwan in 1940 and whose experiences were shaped by Japanese colonialism and the harsh take-over of the KMT are more inclined today to preserve and promote Taiwan autonomy; while the *waishengren*, by comparison "late-comers" and "outsiders," are more likely to adhere to the idea of reunification, as in the Cold War days with their promise of a belated glory to be won by the KMT upon its return to the mainland (cf. p.60). A delicate power play can be seen beneath such labeling and ideological orientation. Mainlanders feared that their fate hinged on the KMT remaining in control as the ruling party in Taiwan. They worried that if the Taiwanese opposition gained control, they would rapidly begin to feel the minority status the KMT shielded them from for so many decades (ibid).

In contrast to Wachman's account of the social and political differences between the *benshengren* and *waishengren* since the mid 1940s, Chang (2003) stresses the critical political consequences of being a "quintessential" Taiwanese, a view shared by some of Taiwanese radicals who chose to flee after the first clashes with the KMT administration after 1945. He observes that for the many Taiwanese who went abroad and became expatriates, Taiwanese nationalism entered a new era. For them, Taiwan now had to aim to be an independent country. Taiwan would have to become "of, by and for" the Taiwan people. Dissident exiles used Tokyo first, and later Washington as home bases to regroup and launch the present-day Taiwanese independence movement (cf. ibid, p. 43).

Self-determination and national independence had been features of the political platform of the Taiwan Communist Party in late 1920s, but the Communists had had precious little chance to promote it in public. Now it became a popular idea with many Taiwanese exiles worldwide because of the tragedies associated with reunification and rebellion. Though the exiles' movement was also divided between left and right and every degree of factional difference, overall the call for self-determination, for a categorical Taiwanese identity completely opposed to Chinese identity, was clearly conceived (ibid). Chang's insights help us understand some of the DPP presidential candidates who had personally experienced exile and their views on the meaning of being Taiwanese and the future for Taiwan.[11]

A series of events in the 1970s further brought complexities to the meaning of Taiwaneseness. For example, overwhelming pressure after 1970 for assimilation, and the contrary opposition movement against authoritarianism, helped crystallize the concepts of "authentic Taiwanese" as opposed to "nationalistic Chinese" (Chang 2003, p.54). This is evident in considering that a strong Chinese identification had been the KMT's trump card when consolidating the post-Japanese Taiwan ethos through attempts to purge the island of Japanese influence and bring legitimacy to KMT rule in Taiwan. With the shift of diplomatic ties involving the UN and the U.S. in the 1970s and the subsequent increasing international isolation that came in its wake, the KMT administration instituted ever more stringent and oppressive policies, even with regard to the party's determination to "reunite with the mainland." In contrast, the DPP promoted a separate Taiwanese identity, winning voters who saw Taiwan as having a distinct colonial past, a history of more progressive economic development, and a young and vibrant democracy. Between the two extreme political outlooks, observers with more pragmatic concerns noted with dismay China's increasingly hostile attitude toward the idea of Taiwan independence and Taiwan's increasing economic dependence on China's huge market and cheap labor. In fact, a different kind of "identity politics"—neither a total identification with everything Chinese nor a complete rejection of Chineseness—entered the political discourse. For example, in various policy statements, high administration officials began to use the term "ethnic Chinese" (*huaren*), rather than "Chinese" (*zhongguoren*) to emphasize the distinction between Taiwanese and Chinese (cf. Ho and Liu 2002).

The shift from politically Chinese to culturally Chinese is not a DPP invention. Tu Wei-ming (1994) points out that *huaren* is not geopolitically centered, only indicating a common ancestry and shared cultural background, whereas *zhongguoren* necessarily evokes obligations and loyalties of political affiliation and the myth of the Central Country. By emphasizing cultural roots, Chinese intellectuals in Taiwan, Hong Kong, and North America hoped to build a transnational network to explore the meaning of being Chinese in a global context (1994, p.31). Efforts to forge a cultural Chinese identity came to constitute a strategy to maintain a critical distance from the official anti-Communist line of the KMT.

Along similar lines but with a more strategic purpose, former president Lee Teng-hui coined the term "New Taiwanese" first in August 1995 in a speech given to the KMT after being chosen as the candidate for the 1996 presidential election. It was a term that he explained in careful wording as "The New Taiwanese conception" (*xin taiwanren guan*). For him, it meant "abandoning divisions based on who arrived first or later" (*xianlai, houdao*) and stressing instead "the love of Taiwan" and the "efforts made for Taiwan," but still retaining the idea that Taiwanese were Chinese and that they "should not forget ultimate reunification."[12] He used the term "New Taiwanese" again while campaigning for mayoral candidate Ma Ying-jeou in 1998. On December 5, 1998, Lee Teng-hui questioned in Tai-yu Ma Ying-jeou, the KMT candidate for Taipei mayor race. Their exchange in Tai-yu on the Taiwan identity issue was so intriguing that we think it would be best to present the question and response here again for the readers to see the full ramifications of such an unusual act by KMT members. The exchange began with Lee asking, "Ma Ying-jeou, where do you come from?" (*Ma Eng-kiu, li si to-ui e lang?*), to which the latter replied "spontaneously" in Tai-yu as follows:

Po-ko Li Chong-tong, goa si lim tai-oan chui, chiah Tai-oan be e sin Tai-oan-lang. Bang-kah chhut-sin e chin-chian e Tai-pak-lang. (Here's my report to President Lee: I am a New Taiwanese who grew up drinking Taiwan water and eating Taiwanese rice, a true Taipei-nese born in Wanhua.[13]

Our analyses will never top the ingenuity of the politicians but the term New Taiwanese as used does get one out of either of the twin traps posed by the DPP's independence platform and the KMT's unification policy by offering a more inclusive group identification for the Taiwan people, especially in comparison with terms such as "Taiwanese" (*benshengren*) and "Mainlanders" (*waishengren*). Under the label "New Taiwanese," all people identifying with the welfare of Taiwan could be included, thus breaking the old ethnolinguistic boundaries.

In addition to the competing nationalistic ideologies generated by the Japanese, the CCP, the KMT and the DPP, the intangible issue of ethnicity or ethnic consciousness has also been high on the political agenda as more interest groups have come forward to contend for power and representation. According to Chang (2003) the ethnicization of politics evolved from the previous Mainlander (*waishengren*) vs. Taiwanese (*benshengren*) paradigm toward a more fine-tuned ethnolinguistic division which is now inextricably intertwined with electoral mobilization and social justice rhetoric in political competition (2003, p. 29). The distinctive ways of grouping people according to a monolithic ethnolinguistic line have since the late 1980s given way to "indigenization" political schemes, paving the way for many social and cultural developments. From the imagined community envisioned by nationalists to imagined divisions dwelled on by radicals, people in Taiwan are discovering new ways of looking at themselves and at others, and are finding new meanings in the speaking of Mandarin and other Chinese varieties. Pluralistic identities implied by the languages they choose to speak are laudable, since language was among the most repressing and repressed symbols during the colonial periods. To bring more objectivity to our point, we first turn to a similar situation in a different locale, where opposition to an English-only ideology has been vocal and has produced a language choice situation quite interesting to aspiring professionals.

Language Choice in Another Socio-political Context

Monica Heller (1988) presents a case in Montreal where French is replacing English as the language of the workplace and where anglophone management and French labor have been turned upside down as a result of a long ethnolinguistic struggle between anglophones and francophones. Her study proposes that codeswitching, i.e., switching back and forth between French and English to a certain extent, is not only a conversational strategy, especially during the beginning and closing of a dialogue where codeswitching can serve as a symbolic act to include participants who speak either of the two languages; it is also an interpersonal management strategy, since switching between French and English as situations demand can sometimes ease tensions and thus maintain harmony. We find that Heller's conclusions and concerns in the Montreal case bear a resemblance to the situation in Taiwan since, like Montreal, Taiwan is going through a succession of social, economic and political changes which bear profound consequences for the meaning of speaking, writing and being in accord with a particular language group[14] in circumstances of rapid democratization and a growing consciousness of national identity.

The Montreal case is typical of how power struggles between different groups can bring changes to the meaning of speaking a certain language, in this case French or English. Two patterns of codeswitching—both, as we shall see, casting further light on the situation in Taiwan—arise. First, making a language choice can be for aspiring professionals a managerial skill to make friends and appease foes in contexts where historical animosities may prevail. Second, making such a choice can also be seen as a political strategy in order to demand rights and representation.

In the Montreal study's first group, newly recruited anglophones hired from other provinces to work in Montreal exhibit interesting patterns of language choice. They have not been part of the long, hard ethnolinguistic struggle and need to demonstrate their French ability in order to stay. For them, codeswitching, i.e., alternating between English and French, is a linguistic necessity and strategy to gain access to both groups without having to take on the full responsibilities and obligations of being either "French" or "English." The other group is made up of young, newly promoted francophones at the management level. They need to use French to establish the new order of power and legitimacy, but they also need to win over the more senior, more experienced anglophones who are blocked from promotion based on their lack of French proficiency. Language choice for them is not only a way to claim legitimacy but also a strategy to neutralize conflict.

The Montreal case parallels the situation of ethnolinguistic struggle in Taiwan, especially among those who see the use and establishment of Tai-yu as a welcome challenge to the authority of Mandarin. Acts of at least symbolic insurrection, often involving the use of Tai-yu, have become increasingly prevalent as demands for democratization have increased and the DPP has tried to challenge the authority of the KMT with strategies designed to "push the boundary of violence"[15] (i.e. use brinkmanship). The lifting of martial law in 1987 brought with it unprecedented freedom and many became more aware of rights they felt they deserved. Among those, the right to mother tongue education became a much debated, much promoted issue among educators. According to Tse (2000), "With reference to language policy and language use, Mandarin remains strong as the national language and a de facto lingua franca. But at the same time, Tai-yu, Hakka, and the native Austro-Polynesian languages have also received increasing attention from the government. Policies for mother-tongue education, bilingual education, and the preservation of endangered varieties of aboriginal languages were designed and implemented with the blessing of the majority of the people" (p.156).

Referring again to the Montreal situation, using Tai-yu in Taiwan public domains such as the workplace became very much like speaking French in Montreal, i.e., to establish a new order of power and legitimacy. This became especially true after the DPP's replacement of the KMT as the ruling party in the 2000 presidential election. When those who did not share the DPP's sociopolitical aspirations but wanted to smooth increasing ethnic tensions began alternating between Mandarin and Tai-yu, that looked like the switching between French and English in Montreal because it was a symbolic gesture, a pledging of allegiance to both groups without subscribing to the full course of ideological contention.

In Montreal the young, newly promoted francophone managers could be likened to aspiring politicians[16] in Taiwan who saw the potential of using either Mandarin or Tai-yu to address constituents of opposed political ideologies—constituents who were now all considering language a requirement for legitimacy and representation. The politicians' use of Mandarin or Tai-yu or both, as situations dictated, was not only a symbolic act to make friends and appease foes but also a management strategy to avoid confrontation and neutralize conflicts.

Heller (1992) focuses on the distribution and functioning of codeswitching as a means of reconstituting social power relations. She does so especially through a re-evaluation of the value of symbolic resources. Thus, the French and English languages are linked in their role of regulating access to other valued symbolic and material resources (1992, p.128). We find Heller's accounts of a surge in the amount of French spoken in areas such as Quebec, and of using French as a way to challenge the dominance of English, most relevant to the situation in Taiwan. Violating the prevailing conventions of language choice is seen as a political strategy to reinforce ethnic boundaries. As an explicit strategy, this was current in the mobilizing of francophones in Quebec in the 1970s, and remains current in mobilizing Ontario francophones today (ibid, p.131).

Heller's study brings two new perspectives to the study of codeswitching in a contested socio-political context. The first is language choice as a political strategy for ethnic mobilization, where the distribution and use of a certain language, such as French or English in Canada, or Mandarin or Tai-yu in Taiwan, can reveal not only the stability of inter-group relations, but also reveal the ways that regulation of access to symbolic resources is tied to the regulation of access to material ones. The second perspective is that language choice as a political strategy for ethnic mobilization can be used to generate momentum and raise consciousness for an ethnic identity by way of a designated linguistic variety in a multilingual and multi-ethnic community. Yet, at the same time, the choice and use of a certain linguistic variety will also open up competition and invite contention, thus running the risk of reinforcing negative discrimination against less privileged groups. What we need to keep in mind is that in the Canadian situation, French is now set up in parallel to English as a crucial linguistic resource to which not only powerful anglophones may aspire, but also relatively powerless groups such as members of native groups and immigrants. What this does, of course, is to create the very kinds of social inequalities within francophone society against which mobilization was directed in the broader frame of Canadian society (Heller 1992, p.139). We shall bring up these two points again when we turn our attention to the ethnolinguistic struggle in Taiwan in Chapter 5 and Chapter 6.

Ambiguities in Language Choice

Issues of intent and meaning in codeswitching have always been debated by scholars of codeswitching. For example, Stroud (1992) points out that it was quite simply not possible to confidently attribute any specific meanings to particular code switches, and that any single switch could be performing a number of different functions. Stroud further argues that this ambiguity and indeterminacy is not incidental but is one of the most salient and central characteristics of codeswitching, and is typical of how speech is handled generally. Li (1998) studies the hows and whys in codeswitching based on data and theories from conversation analysis. Not all language choice and use is rational, nor is the speaker's intention is always conscious. Such cases are more salient in daily conversations among lay persons, where language proficiency, ease of communication, and expressions of professionalism may all take precedence over cost-benefit calculations. For example, even native Taiwanese whose Tai-yu is better overall than their Mandarin sometimes command political terminology better in Mandarin than in Tai-yu. However, in our study we focus on the political rhetoric of presidential candidates during TV debates, a form of discourse where personal and political stakes are high and diplomacy and strategy are called for. In this context, ambiguities and uncertainty seem to be all the more important when speakers try to convey sensitive issues such as national identity while at the same time seeking to preserve peace and solidarity with most voters. For our analysis, we will take up the proposal of Heller (1988) and use markedness theory and Bakhtinian notions of translinguistics and dialogue to analyze uncertainty in language choice occurring in political discourse.

Heller (1988) discusses reasons why language choice may work as a strategy both in situations of certainty and of uncertainty—that is, (a) in situations where clear, unmarked conventions of language choice may be found; and (b) in situations where no such conventions may exist or where there may be competing conventions (1988, p. 81). She further hypothesizes that language choice can create ambiguities either by violating conventional associations (without redefining them), by refusing to define them (where they do not exist), or by refusing to choose among them (where several frames of references are in competition) (ibid, p. 82).

Ambiguities and uncertainty in a language choice in a specific context can work effectively in managing conflicts (since speakers are merely making inferences without putting themselves on record) and in enacting symbolic roles. In the Taiwanese political context, the meaning of a language choice can derive from a context other than the pragmatic/functional context, and can be linked to conflicting ideologies over Chinese/Taiwanese—the former ideologies premised, as mentioned, on cultural-historical determinacy, the latter on political pragmatism.

The Bakhtinian notion of "translinguistics" is useful to our understanding of language choice, for it allows us to see language as an ideological site where conflicting voices (opinions and discussions internalized prior to the encounter or discourse taking place) come into play. The notion further permits us to analyze language choice because we can see that the speaker is trying to choose from opposing ideologies and is admitting the possibility for dominance (Bakhtin 1981; Hill and Hill 1986). These concepts moreover allow us to study speakers' adjustments to uncertainty in fluid speech communities. Finally, the framework allows us to see verbal behavior as relations of force between speakers.

In sum, inferences that can be made about a language choice in a contested political context are very much a useful thing since they can permit speakers to say and do, and indeed be, two or more things where normally a choice is expected. They allow speakers to take refuge in the voice of the other in order to say or do things that they normally wouldn't be able to get away with, and they also allow speakers to assert their own voice to claim new roles, new rights and new obligations (Heller 1988, p. 93). Moreover, we argue that politicians, who want to polarize issues, instill fear or stir up emotions, yet at the same time preserve their rapport with other constituents, might also adopt code switching as a preferred strategy to win friends and appease foes.

In the following section we will look at more individual politicians and their choices and the use of language in political discourse to provide further examples of language use in power struggles.

Texts and Discussions

The following excerpts are taken from the 1995 presidential television debates among four DPP nominees. As the structure of the debates was set, each nominee first presented a seven-minute speech that was followed by questions from media representatives. The question and answer sessions were extended in order to solicit a wider spectrum of opinions. The moderator used Tai-yu throughout the entire debate; most of the nominees used Tai-yu in their opening remarks, except Lin Yi-hsiung who opted to use Mandarin throughout his entire opening speech.[17] During the question and answer sessions the media representative opted to use either Mandarin or Tai-yu depending on the type of question and the presumed ideological stance. For example, the *People's Daily*, a supporter of the DPP, used Tai-yu to pose the question of whether there was such a thing as the "politicized ethnic issue." The *China Times*, which took a relatively more neutral position, asked the candidates in Mandarin what the future president's top priorities for the twenty-first century should be. The nominees when answering opted for either Mandarin or Tai-yu as they saw fit.

Our first excerpt is from Hsu Hsing-liang's response to the question by the chief editor of *The People's Daily*. The editor, Lee Wong-tai, asked if there was a "politicized ethnic issue" (cheng3-ti7 siang7 e5 chok8-kun5 bun7-te5) accompanying Taiwan's liberalization, and he further asked if Hsu, who is ethnically Hakka, had ever experienced discrimination.

The following is part of Hsu's response:
goa it9 tit jin3 ui5, tai7 oan5 e7 chok kun5 bun3 te5, ki7 pun siong3 si3 keN7 che2 bun3 te5, put9 si7 jin3 tong7 a2 si3 thong tok8 bun3 te5; si3 kong goa3 seng2 chok kun5 si3 an2 na e3 keng7 lan2 bin7 chin2 tong2 chip9 cheng3 leh? sit chai3 si3 u3 kau2 kan tan, i7 tiong7 ki5 i lai5 kho2 kok9 bin7 tong2 chia9 png7, i7 hoan7 lo kong, jiok si3 lan bin7 chin2 tong2 chip9 cheng, i7 si3 put9 si7 ke2 siok e3 tit9 tio3 che cheng2 po chiong3? sou i lan chai3 chhu2, jiok si3 be2 soan chong thong2, lan u3 pit9 iau2 hoe7 choan7 the2 tai7 oan5 jin7 bin5 po cheng3, lan jiok si3 chip9 cheng3, lan be2 ka3 tai7 oan5 mui2 chit8 ko2 jin7 chun7 giam5, seng7 chun7 e7 koan7 li7. chhiouN7, kejia, lan kheh lang7 la, goa siong7 sin2 che ki7 pun siong3 si3 bun7 hoa3 e7 bun3 te5, tio3 si3 gi gian5 e7 bun3 te5 chio sou3 bin7 chok8 e7 gi gian5 bun7 hoa3, iau2 i2 kok9 ka lek liong7 ke7 i po hou7, che si3 kok9 ka tiong3 iau3 e7 chu7 san2. ki7 thaN e7 bun3 te5 chai7 tai7 oan5, hoan tng2 put9 siuN7 tiong3 iau3, li2 ong3 tai5 e3 siuN7, lan hi sin2 liong5 si7 kejiaren, si3 m3 si3 lang3 e3 tui2 li u3 phian7 kian3, tai7 oan5 si3 chiok chengshou e sia3 hoe7, but che cheng phian7 kian3.

Trans
I have always thought that the ethnic issue in Taiwan is an economic issue; it is not an identity issue or a unification/independence issue. Why are the Mainlanders afraid of us, the DPP, governing (the country)? This is simple. The KMT has been their meal ticket for a long time and they are afraid that if the DPP takes over power, then they might not continue to have such privilege. Therefore, we should promise to the people in Taiwan, if the DPP governs, we will provide everybody the right to live in a dignified way. . . . As for Hakka, we the Hakka, I believe this is a cultural issue and a language issue. We should use government

resources to protect the culture and language of the minorities. They are great resources for the country. [Other than this,] there are not that many problems in Taiwan. Lee Wong-tai might think that Hsu Hsing-liang is Hakka[18]; would he be prejudiced against you? Taiwan is a very mature society; there is no such prejudice.

In this excerpt Hsu, who twice served the DPP as chairman, is responding to the question of whether there really is such a thing as a "politicized ethnic issue" accompanying Taiwan's liberalization. The chief editor, Lee Wong-tai of the *People's Daily*, a pro-DPP newspaper, asked the question in Taiwanese. Hsu's response was mostly in Tai-yu, a we-code that symbolizes solidarity among DPP supporters. He offers an account of why the "ethnic issue" is not a political issue but an economic one, soothing KMT supporters who might be afraid of losing long-enjoyed advantages if they (the KMT supporters) switched allegiance. He further claims that "ethnic issues" among the minorities are cultural and language issues.

In terms of language choice, Hsu opted to use Mandarin twice for the same expression, Hakka, one of the ethnic minorities in Taiwan. Since setting, topic and participants all remain unchanged in this long response, we find no motives of situational switching (Gumperz 1982). However, the marked choice of using Mandarin for "Hakka" does carry metaphorical weight. Under markedness theory, Hsu's choice of Mandarin should serve as a symbolic gesture to negotiate a different set of responsibilities and obligations. Choosing Mandarin to enunciate the word Hakka can be seen as adopting a they-code, which not only interrupts Hsu's fluent Tai-yu but also alienates Hsu as a member of the "minority." This is further evidenced when Hsu immediately switches back to Tai-yu and uses expressions such as "we the Hakka" to renegotiate his right and obligation as one of "us" and one of "the Hakka." The rational choice (RC) theory offers a further account of Hsu's two switches to Mandarin and back to Tai-yu within consecutive items. The they-code "Mandarin" for Hakka helped Hsu underscore the alienation and estrangement of the "minority," and the we-code "Taiwanese" to express "we the Hakka" helped identify Hsu as a DPP leader who thinks that the "minority issue" is a cultural and language issue. Hsu's "rational choice" of Mandarin helped him renegotiate his right and obligation as a minority and a DPP leader and invoked a maximally authentic "minority" among the DPP members and supporters. For Hsu, alternating between Mandarin and Tai-yu was a linguistic necessity and a strategy to gain access to both groups without having to take the full responsibility and obligations of being either "Chinese" or "Hakka."

The following excerpt is the response of Peng Ming-min to a question from the chief editor of the *China Times* on top priorities for the future president in approaching the twenty-first century.

Excerpt
chit9 ma2 tai7 oan5 e7 sia3 hoe7, si7 chit8 ko3 be5-sit tek sia7-hoe7, mishi de shehui, hun7-to lang5 tou chai7 mng7, dau2 de che ko2 cheng2 hu2, be2 cha2

gun2 kau2 siaN mih hong7 hiong3 ? sou i chai3 che ko2 gi7 bun3 e7, jim3 ho5 chiong7 lai5 e7 chong thong2, siang3 kin7 pun2 e7 lim3 bu7 u3 liong ko3: te7 chit8 kok9 ka e7 toa7 hong7 hiong3, gun be2 kiaN7 kau2 to ui7, be2 kong tek9 hun3 chheng7 chho ka3 kok9 bin5 liau kai2; women shi shei? Taiwan shi shenme? Weishenme women yao zai zheli? Women yao xiang nali zou? che tio3 si3 siang3 tiong3 iau2 e, pau7 koat9 kok9 ka e7 teng3 ui7.

Trans
Contemporary Taiwan is a lost society. A lot of *people are* wondering where this government is taking us. In this uncertainty lie two fundamental tasks for the future president: first, he has to point out clearly the direction of the country to the people. Who are we? What is Taiwan? Why are we here? Where are we going? This is the most important task, involving as it does the identity of the nation.

In this excerpt, Peng, like all of the DPP candidates, used the unmarked, we-code (Tai-yu) to answer the question about the top priorities for the future president in the twenty-first century. Peng stated that contemporary Taiwan is a lost society, and he stressed this by repeating "lost society" first in Tai-yu and then in Mandarin, a marked choice, which interrupts Peng's fluent stream of Tai-yu and draws attention to Peng's emphasis on the state of Taiwan society. Using codeswitching as a pragmatic strategy to draw attention and to repeat an important message is very common among politicians as well as advertisers (Wei, 2003). Gumperz (1982) points out that reiteration is among the conversational functions of codeswitching. In some cases, repetition may serve to clarify what is said, but often it simply amplifies or emphasizes a message (1982, p.78). When a catchword or phrase is expressed in one language, repeated in a second, and reiterated in another if necessary, it not only helps the speaker achieve emphasis but also helps the audience remember the point.

Peng's second switch to Mandarin in the same response carries more metaphorical weight and is best explained by the ideas of "voice," "dialogue" and "translinguistic" model as proposed by M. M. Bakhtin (1981). The identification of "voices" and an account of the theoretical possibilities for the juxtaposition of voices are major concerns in translinguistics. The choice of code, that is, of language, in code switching can be seen as just one aspect of the many ways in which voices can be different from each other (Hill and Hill 1986, p. 388). Under the framework of the translinguistic model, what we stress is the fluidity and possibility of different "voices" entering a stream of words from the speaker. In contrast, the traditional code switch model, although it admits the pragmatic function of a language choice, still puts an emphasis on the coherence of the language structure. Thereby we identify constraints and rules of when and why a certain switch can't occur in a sentence, but we are denied the chance of allowing conflicting analyses of the same code or considering the possibility that the speaker is accommodating seemingly opposed ideologies. The translinguistic model lets us see the interaction of different codes as voices interacting with and struggling against each other. Such a model, applied to words and phrases, goes beyond the traditional linguistic sense, entering the realm of a speaker's consciousness where the focus is no longer on coherence in language structure or straightforward matching among various choices and their pragmatic functions. Instead, a dialogue is seen where different if not conflicting voices representing opposing ideologies struggle to dominate, and where the speaker is trying to adopt both the authorial voice and the embedded voice for purposes of ideological dueling.

Returning to the Peng example, in discussing top priorities for the future president he stresses that Taiwan is a lost society because the people are unsure of the direction of the KMT government. Peng's contention about the identity of the nation is best explained in Rigger (1997), where the author traces the sources for such contentions and stresses the irrevocable differences in perspective between the DPP and the KMT on the question of Taiwan's future status. According to Rigger, supporters of unification and supporters of Taiwan independence each view Taiwan's status through radically different logical frameworks. Unification supporters are guided by historical determinism. They believe that because Taiwan was part of China in the past, and because the island's residents have ancestral ties to mainland China, Taiwan is therefore an unalienable part of Chinese territory that must be brought under the control of the mainland Chinese state. In contrast, advocates of Taiwan independence are guided by the logic of pragmatism. In their view, cultural identity does not dictate political identity, and decisions about Taiwan's status should be guided by the will of the island's people rather than by an abstract notion of historic destiny. Today, this logic serves Taiwan independence supporters seeking to redefine Taiwan as a political entity separate from the mainland Chinese state (ibid).

Understanding through Rigger the sources of Taiwan contention and its intransigence helps shed light on Peng's codeswitching between Tai-yu and Mandarin. Peng chooses Mandarin to ask himself a series of questions—"Who are we?" "What is Taiwan?" "Why are we here?" "Where are we going?" After he is done with these interrogatives, he switches to Tai-yu once again to answer, concluding that formulating a national identity is the most important task. If we approach Peng's seeming soliloquy through Bakhtin's translinguistic framework, we see not just that Mandarin interrupts a stream of Tai-yu for the sake of posing rhetorical questions, or that it establishes a clear dichotomy between the we-code and they-code to renegotiate a new set of responsibilities and obligations for the speaker. Rather, Peng tries to use both Mandarin and Tai-yu to create a sort of dialogue between conflicting ideologies—that of the incumbent KMT advocating unification and submission to the pressure of Beijing, as opposed to the conviction of the DPP challengers that autonomy would be best for Taiwan. Further presenting the two conflicting ideologies are the very metonymic associations of the two languages—Mandarin, official and authoritative, and Tai-yu, the language of democracy and the people; the one suggesting Chinese, the other Taiwanese; the one the voice of unification, the other bespeaking separation. The essence of the exchange is not dictated by grammar or function. Instead, it is defined by the volatile dominance of conflicting ideologies. In summary,

Bakhtin's theory allows Peng to confront different language choices in a context of struggle for power. Concepts such as "voices" and "dialogue" further transform seeming soliloquy into dialogue. The interaction becomes not a simple disruption, but a translinguistic battlefield upon which two ways of speaking struggle for dominance.

In another debate excerpt, the problem of Taiwan identity reverberates with foreign relations aspects. Lin Yi-hsiung was responding to a question about how he viewed the KMT's "practical diplomacy." The question was put to him by the chief editor of the *Taiwan Times*, a pro-DPP newspaper published in Taiwanese. Lin begins his answer in Tai-yu, alternates to Mandarin and switches back to Tai-yu in conclusion. He blames the KMT "practical diplomacy" for trapping Taiwan in a "One-China" framework, stressing the importance of treating Taiwan as Taiwan and China as China.

Excerpt
i it-tit8 loh8-jip8 chit8 lei3 tiong-kok tek kheng-kheng lai7, i put kaN2 beng5-cheng3-gian5-sun7, ming-cheng-yan-shun, **ming-cheng-yan-shun** de ba Taiwan dangcheng yige guojia, suoyi minjindang yao tupuo waijiao de kunjing zui zhuyaode shi ba Taiwan dang Taiwan, ba Zhongguo dang Zhongguo. dei7 che kuang2 cheng5-heng5 e7, kok-che3 sia7-hoe7 chiah e7 kam2-kak li2 si7 chit8 lei3 tok8-lip8 e kok-ka, Tai5-oan5 kah Tiong-kok e5 bun7-te5, chiah e7 pian3-seng5 kok-che3-hoa3 e5 bun7-te5。chit8 lei3 tiong-kok cheng3-chhek e chhok-gou7, bok8-cheng5 soushuode wushi waijiao genben bu wushi, lian mingzi dou bu shizai, hai shuo shenme waijiao? sou2-i2 beh kai2-koat Tai5-oan5 e5 bun7-te5, pit-su chiong kok-bin5-tong2 oaN7-lo-lai5。

Trans
They [the KMT] have fallen into the trap of the "One China" framework. They dare not ratify Taiwan as a nation.[19] Therefore, the most important diplomatic breakthrough for the DPP is to treat Taiwan as Taiwan, China as China. Under this circumstance, international society will treat you as an independent nation; the issue between China and Taiwan will be an international issue.... The mistake of the One China policy [is that] the diplomacy we have is not practical at all; even the name is not real, not to mention the diplomacy. Therefore, the solution to the Taiwan issue is to replace the KMT regime.

Lin's remarks essentialize the fundamental difference between the DPP and the KMT on China policy. For the DPP, the underlying principle of that policy can be characterized as "One China, One Taiwan." That is, "Taiwan is an independent and sovereign state; it does not belong to the People's Republic of China and it has no sovereign power over the Chinese mainland." This principle is a manifestation of the DPP's commitment to Taiwanese nationalism and is in direct conflict with the mainland Chinese position on Taiwan's identity (Rigger 1997; Wachman 1994a, 1994b; Wang 2000).

The DPP assertion that Taiwan deserves statehood separate from China, it should be noted, is built on the party's understanding of the term "Chinese." For many DPP leaders, the term "Chinese" referring to people is considered only a cultural or ethnic specification of *huaren*, not a political designation. That is, they are willing to identify themselves as Chinese in a cultural or ethnic sense, but see themselves as citizens of Taiwan. The idea that all Chinese must live under the same government is likewise rejected. From there it is logical to argue that Taiwan deserves separate statehood. Citing the UN Charter and other international agreements, the DPP argues that self-determination is a fundamental principle in the modern international system. Taiwan's residents should have the right to decide in an island-wide referendum whether the establishment of the "Republic of Taiwan" and the adoption of a new constitution are warranted. Any interference with the right to make these political choices is considered a violation of the principle of self-determination. The DPP thus rejects both versions of the "One China" framework as proposed by Beijing and by the KMT (Wang 2000).

According to Chu (2000), the problem of identity ambiguity that has beset Taiwan in both its domestic and foreign relations politics is further complicated by three other significant factors: the failure of the KMT leadership to define a new national identity, the rapid transformation of a natively-oriented Taiwanese consciousness from a counter-hegemonic critique of the KMT China-oriented identity to a dominant ideology, and the rising visibility of Taiwan in the international community due to its economic success (2000, p. 303).

In terms of language choice, we find that Lin's juxtaposing Mandarin and Tai-yu indicates metaphorically the authority of his statement and the struggle for means, recognition, and identity. Using Mandarin helps lend authority and objectification to the importance of the ratification of Taiwan as a nation. It also serves as an "internal polemic" voice, in which we can see Lin (and the DPP membership) struggling against the very necessary words and the ideology they imply (cf. Hill and Hill 1986, p. 393). Shifting between Mandarin and Tai-yu in this context serves not to neutralize ethnic boundaries or to reinforce them. Rather, it is a political strategy to present the contesting ideologies between the DPP and the KMT, each representing an opposing view on national diplomacy and sovereignty.

Conclusion

In this chapter, we have provided accounts of the study of language choices as they relate to power struggles. The Montreal case by Heller (1988) offers inspiration and brings up parallels for how the making of a language choice can be an acquired socio-political skill in a contested context. As with speakers of English and French in Montreal, many Taiwan speakers have experienced the contested meaning of speaking a language and have learned to adopt codeswitching as a way to get on with daily linguistic transactions. However, unlike Montreal, Taiwan has a volatile relationship with China, which only recognizes an essentializing model of one language/one nation/one state, making issues such as language choices as they relate to identity politics worse than threatening and thus demanding more in the way of strategies. The uncertain meanings of a national language (Japanese, Mandarin, or Tai-yu) and a national identity (Japanese, Chinese, or Taiwanese) require more than a functional or a socio-pragmatic approach. It is this aspect which makes the issue of language choice in Taiwan more politically acute than in places such as Montreal.

The 1995 televised DPP presidential campaign speeches and Bakhtin's notions of translinguistic, voices and dialogue provide possibilities for admitting conflicting ideologies. Furthermore, critical issues such as ethnic boundaries, national identity and diplomacy are argued and presented according to the candidates' choice and use of either Mandarin or Tai-yu. Our three excerpts serve as pertinent examples to illustrate how language choice can serve as a necessary political strategy to gain access to a specific group without undertaking the full responsibilities and obligations of "being" a member of the group. Under Bakhtin's translinguistic framework, language choice can further be seen as a dialogue where conflicting voices struggle for legitimacy and representation. In addition, alternating between Mandarin and Tai-yu can bring a fuller picture of contentions and tensions in national diplomacy, where conflicting views are proposed by the KMT and the DPP.

Implications

The premise of this chapter rests on language choice being seen as related to power struggle. Such a relationship is especially prominent when viewing Taiwan's colonial past, where the Japanese, Chinese, and Taiwanese have all used language (Japanese, Mandarin, and Tai-yu) to establish nationalism and patriotism, inculcate people with the values of civility and high culture, and heighten the sense of democracy and pride in a mother tongue. The Taiwan situation is no exception to other communities such as Montreal, in which migrations and changing social structures and relations of power have transformed language choice and practice.

The three politicians' choice and use of Mandarin and Tai-yu can serve as a case study of how aspiring politicians see language as a vital means for ethnic mobilization and as a challenge to the existing order of legitimacy and representation. What the Taiwanese politicians are doing bears resemblance to the situation in Canada where newly promoted anglophones in Montreal see choosing and using French as a way to gain upward mobility, and where young aspiring francophones promoted to managerial levels see the necessity to use English at least occasionally to appease tension and gain friendship. Nevertheless, the Taiwan situation bears one more critical concern—Taiwan's relationship with China, with the latter threatening a military assault should independence be declared.

Puzzles remain. Why do questions such as an exclusive ethnicity, official language or competing nationalistic visions persist despite their logical flaws and impracticality? Why in the day of emerging democracy do people still use splitting strategies such as us/them to get to the voters, use socially hierarchical values such as discrimination/subordination to understand ethnic relations, and use the threat of war to muster ethos and morale? The simplest answer is that these are just election tactics, but we have learned much more from the juxtapositions of Mandarin and Tai-yu by the three presidential hopefuls and by consulting Taiwan's colonial past. Moreover, as we learned from the works of Bakhtin, Ching, and Chang, and from Heller's findings, socio-political contingencies and pluralities offer better concepts for understanding issues such as identities, language choices and power struggles. As the DPP gained power, multilingualism and multiculturalism became platforms that helped implement programs such as mother tongue language instruction and the multicultural curriculum. Tai-yu is not likely to replace Mandarin as the official language; rather, English is the choice of most for consideration as a second official language, not for its neutral ethnic position as some would assume, but for the economic and international status associated with it. The juxtaposed usage of Mandarin and Tai-yu, accompanied with contesting nationalistic/pragmatic ideologies, might be seen as ways to imagine Taiwan's future.

In the next chapter, we look into the evolution and formation of language policy-making. We examine the ideology behind the power struggles and decision-making and argue that narratives for promoting or abolishing a certain form of language policy—assimilationism, pluralism, multiculturalism—tend to become emotionally charged as they concern not only language per se, but how policy envisions and enacts ties of language to identity, morality and epistemology. Moreover, we point out that language policy in a multicultural context implies conflict and controversy as it becomes the object of contention not only over symbolic recognition of minorities but also over the appropriation of educational resources and the status to be granted linguistic diversity.

Notes

1. According to Wachman (1994, p.108), in the very earliest years after the KMT arrived, teachers still used both Mandarin and Tai-yu to explain material in class. But in 1953, the government required that either Tai-yu or Chinese be used as the language of instruction, and in 1964 a law was passed forbidding the use of Tai-yu in schools or official settings. This was accompanied by a campaign that emphasized the grace of Mandarin and the comparative vulgarity of Tai-yu.

2. The usage of all forms and varieties of Chinese as well as aboriginal languages was formally banned in 1937 by the Japanese administration when the Taiwan governor-general's office launched a total mobilization campaign to transform all Taiwanese into

imperial subjects. This was part of the over-all *Kominka* (assimilation) policy (1937-1945) in order to prepare the people on the island help Japan to fight the war.

3. Such punishment was mostly in schools, and it was mostly minor, involving such things as small fines of money or occasionally a slap on the wrist or other minor physical punishment. The author was schooled in Taipei during the 1970s and never experienced or witnessed such punishment, but later heard about instances of it from friends schooled in other cities.

4. From "Turning Taiwanese," *The Economist*, 01/15/2005, Vol. 374, Issue No. 8409.

5. This refers to the demonstrations that took place in Beijing on May 4, 1919 and the complex emotional, cultural, and political developments that followed. Among some of the most radical ideas relevant to this book flowered then—the replacement of *wenyan* with *baihua* to modernize and unite the country, the subsequent standardization of modern Chinese, and the adoption of democracy.

6. The main issue in the linguistic debate even then was that standardizing pronunciation could not proceed without an agreement on the selection of the written form of the character. Purists insisted on using colloquial pronunciation as the standard in selecting or creating the appropriate character; whereas the reformers suggested Mandarin *baihuawen* as the written character corpus. Of course, the *baihuawen* that Taiwan reformers had in mind featured pronunciation with Taiwan colloquialisms. On the ideological level, the debate promoted the plurality of Chinese language as expressions of Chinese culture, and by doing so, challenged the traditional ideal of a unified Chinese language through script (Heylen 2005, p. 503).

7. For more insights on these movements, please read Peng, Ming-min (1972). *A Taste of Freedom: Memoirs of a Formosan Independence Leader.* New York: Halt, Rinehart & Winston.

8. Land reform was carried out in three stages: (1) rent reduction in 1949 (from around 50 percent to 37.5 percent of the main crop); (2) sale of public lands in 1951 to tenant farmers at 2.5 times the value of one year's crop (resulting in 96,000 hectares of public land going to 156,000 tenant farm families); and (3) the "land-to-the-tiller" program, which forced landlords to sell land they did not farm themselves, except for 2.1 hectares of paddy field and double that amount for dry land (Copper 1996, p. 119). The reform improved agricultural productivity and increased overall production, which was a pre-condition for industrial development. It further equalized the distribution of wealth, income and social status in rural areas and made Taiwan more a land of small, independent farmers, most of whom quickly became integrated into commercial networks. Last, it won the support of many small farmers, and helped to integrate them into the ROC system (cf. Rigger 1999, pp. 68-69).

9. H. M. Tien, and C. J. Shiau, "Taiwan's Democratization: A Summary," *World Affairs* 155, no. 2 (1992): 61.

10. It is important to see that these are two generalized categories and that their resonances are no longer true as the post war generation stepped up interactions and intermarriage. In addition, "Taiwanese" (*benshengren*, literally meaning persons from "this" province) does not refer simply to everyone living in Taiwan. In the sense of people rather than language, it is a term used to denote only Han Chinese living in Taiwan prior to the wave of migration that occurred at the end of the 1940s, and their offspring. The term "Mainlander" (*waishengren*) literally means people from outside of the province and is also used elsewhere in China to denote those who come from another province. The dichotomous notion of labeling people is imprecise and, in any case, is more meaningful

when applied to the generations alive in the 1940s and 1950s than to those born since. Not everyone living in Taiwan fits into one of the two categories, even though it is in terms of these categories that the political debate has been framed (cf. Wachman 1994b, pp.16-17). Between the two groups are the Hakka and aborigines, although together they constitute less than 15 percent of the population (see Chapter 2, section 2).

11. See, for example, Peng, Ming-min (1972). *A Taste of Freedom: Memoirs of a Formosan independence leader*. New York: Holt, Rinehart & Winston.

12. See Stephane Corcuff. (ed.) 2002. *Memories of the Future: National Identity Issues and the Search for a New Taiwan*, pp. 186-87. New York: M. E. Sharpe.

13. The question, translation and transliteration is taken from Corcuff, 2002, p. 187.

14. In Taiwan's case, Mandarin Chinese and/or Tai-yu.

15. One of the most influential DPP activists, Hsu Xing-liang, advocated such a strategy in his book *Bao Li Bian Yuan (The Boundary of Violence)*. The use of Tai-yu, and vulgar Tai-yu at that, in all public domains, even the legislature, was recommended as one of many instances of symbolic violence best calculated to challenge and humiliate authority.

16. This comparison is by no means sarcastic or condescending, as some might think who associate politicians with skillful word manipulation and don't find that generally true among businessmen. We are only interested in using the comparison to point out the importance in Taiwan of speaking more than one language and knowing which one to use or not use in handling potentially tense situations.

17. Since Lin only used Mandarin throughout the entire TV election campaign, we didn't include his speech in our analysis of language choice and identity politics. Of course, this is not to say that Lin was not playing politics with his choice of not responding in Tai-yu.

18. It is interesting to point out that the Hakka are also known for being politically talented. In addition to Hsu, the ex-president Lee Teng-hui, for example, is Hakka.

19. Lin's view of the KMT's national policy as unpractical and his contention that there has not been a Taiwan national policy can be best explained by Muyard (2005). Both the Republic of China (ROC) and People's Republic of China (PRC) are modeled after a Chinese state. There hasn't been a Taiwan Republic after all the years of democratization. The current DPP administration still adopts the name of ROC, though its core political ideology has deviated from the China-center creed and some of its radicals have opted for independence as ideal for Taiwan's future.

Chapter 5
From Nationalism to Multiculturalism: Making Choices in Language Policy

Introduction

In this chapter, we offer a socio-political perspective on the study of language policy and language in education, using Taiwan's experience with the dilemma of a Mandarin-plus or Mandarin-only program as a case in point. This perspective is different from what we presented in previous chapters where language was seen as more or less political symbols, capable of making or breaking cultural/ethnic/national boundaries and subject to manipulations by movers and shakers in the field. Here our goal in presenting various conceptual metaphors is only to present a more rounded view of the socio-political scenes associated with language variations in Taiwan. It is made possible by journeying historically back through Taiwan's language evolution. In the past, a nationalism-driven ideology twice promoted monolingualism in which a non-indigenous minority language policy (Japanese in the first case and Mandarin in the second) was implemented. Subsequently the Mandarin-only, Chinese-centered ideology came under serious attack, mostly by independence-minded political radicals, although counter attacks also were launched by Hakka and aboriginals determined to contest the monopoly of a quintessential Taiwan nationalism. In the midst of these power struggles, issues related to language and identity became heatedly debated. Emerging democracy contributed to a surge of voters mobilized around issues such as ethno-linguistic justice, equality and rights for language minorities, and a (mis)use of language discourse as a proxy war for resources and representation became evident. A pluralistic platform emphasizing rights and equality for language advocates is needed.

In addition, to make a more objective point, we argue that much conviction and sentiment in Taiwan runs parallel to that surrounding the English-plus or English-only debate in the U.S.,[1] with a good deal of the Taiwan contention attributable to political ontological clashes between assimilationists and pluralists over equality and rights, and with national identity politics a strong undercurrent in these discourses. The insistence on having an official language or none at all has much to do with whether we conceptualize language as a practical medium or as an ideological national symbol. Beneath much of the controversy over language or the choice of a language, we are actually asking core questions about who we are, about our attitude toward those who are different from us, and about the role of the state. These are deeply poignant questions, and of course there are no easy answers. The same group that supports bilingual education for immigrants might not want to foot the bill for that as they see their taxes increase. Past experience with minorities and the injustices felt by them may be hard to set aside, but the same advocates for the equality of all might disagree on which language(s) to choose when it comes to staying competitive in a global market. Identity in a post-nationalistic era might not correlate with a national ideology, but the tension between individual and group identity can still be ambiguous and contentious. As we will learn from Taiwan's past and present, as well as from Canadian and U.S. experience with language as a political problem or exploitable resources, a clearer picture of making language choices in a multicultural context is surely needed.

We use comments and editorials from the media as well as official documents to support these views and show that since the beginning of the twenty-first century, Taiwan's Ministry of Education (MOE) has implemented a revised language policy in education with a concentric, more inclusive imprint for national identity. In addition, mother tongue education has become part of the school curriculum and legal framework, and political representation has been adjusted to protect the rights of minority groups. Nevertheless, multiculturalism has met its challenge in the effort to stress equality and rights. Economic rationalism has been the major reason for a mounting popularity of English and Mandarin. Last, we point out that while a liberal language policy alone might provide a forum for different voices, a political structure that institutionalizes equality and prevents domination is also needed for the equal development of multiculturalism.

Contending Forces in a Multicultural Context

In this chapter we try to the highlight the play of forces working over the last few decades for acceptance of a broader range of language diversity in Taiwan. These forces didn't gather without complications and conflict. They came as the result of rapid democratization in an election-driven culture where voters mobilized around several key issues: notably, correction of ethno-linguistic injustice, recalibration of identity politics by way of language diversity in a contested context, and the balancing of multiculturalism with economic rationalism. Our analysis serves a twofold purpose.

On the one hand we want to argue that the language discourse we are facing in Taiwan is unique and certainly not comparable to language discourses in the US. This is because of the conundrum in Taiwan between a nationalistic language policy such as Mandarin-only (the default policy since the KMT's heyday) and support for a Mandarin-plus policy. That is, the twice over monolingualism in Taiwan during the Japanese and KMT administrations resulted in nonindigenous minority languages, i.e. Japanese and Mandarin, being chosen to replace indigenous languages spoken by the majority. To political radicals today, this dubious historical legacy seriously undermines Mandarin's legitimacy to serve as the only official language. Moreover, we argue that what really underlies these heated debates are not only conflicting visions of the dynamics of Taiwan's status quo but also maneuvering for resources and representation among different language groups. With neither a China-center nor a Taiwan independent state seen as viable by most citizens, a language policy promising the most political stability and economic viability is attractive. An economic rationale for language policy implementation might well be presented as an alternative to boost competitiveness in response to globalization. Nevertheless, this approach runs contrary to the anticipation of increasing democratization, which has encouraged rising ethnic consciousness to expect rights and representation in all socio-political aspects.

On the other hand, we also want to point out that there are similarities between the Mandarin-only or Mandarin-plus debates and those of English-only or English-plus in the U.S. In both places much discontent has flowed from two different political thought patterns—the concern of assimilationists for national unity over ethnolinguistic diversification and their vision of using the dominant language (Mandarin or English) to upgrade minorities from an economically and politically subordinate status—and the pluralists' conviction that most societies are fundamentally multicultural and multilingual and that genuine equality can only be achieved by tendering to individuals their rights even at the state's expense.

This chapter is organized as follows: 1) a discussion of making choices in a multicultural situation; 2) an overview of language policy in Taiwan starting from the colonial periods; 3) the changing tide: from imagined community to imagined divisions; 4) the dilemma of a Mandarin-only or Mandarin-plus program; 6) multiculturalism in hindsight.

Managing Choices in a Multicultural Situation

We think of language policy as managing the networking of different languages. Our position is a deliberate attempt to break away from the goal-oriented approach advocated by most of the monolingual nationalistic policies, where the aim is to set up a standard language for all for the purpose of nation building (Fishman 1969, 1972). Under the nationalistic scheme, decisions about language use in public schools, in the delivery of public services, in the courts, in the ballot booth, and so on, are all calculated to further the nation-building objective (cf. Patten 2003, p. 365). Our approach also differs from the language maintenance model, which, in contrast to the previous approach, shifts its priority to the maintenance and protection of particular language communities vulnerable to marginalization or extinction. Under either the language convergence or language maintenance scheme, language choices and functions become a central concern of the state; the making of such choices may be motivated politically or pragmatically. In contrast, we advocate a hybrid of liberal neutrality that maintains national coherence with diversity and takes a non-interfering, non-goal oriented attitude toward competition and contention among interest groups.

Our suggestion is similar to what has been proposed by Patten (2003), who argues that the task of a language policy is not to realize some specific linguistic outcome but to establish fair background conditions under which speakers of different languages can strive for the survival and success of their respective language communities (p. 366). In other words, we should heed the pluralist dilemma where the problem is to reconcile social cohesion (civism) on the one hand and recognize and incorporate ethnic, linguistic and cultural diversity within the nation-state on the other (May 1998, p. 273). To address the full ramifications of this dilemma, we must confront some of the contending issues, namely, the critique of the Mandarin-only policy, the prospects of successor policies in the midst of mounting political pressure from the ruling DPP, and the rising need to grant standing for indigenous languages. At the same time, we must also be concerned with the promotion of mother tongue education, as well as the growing pressures of globalization. We must also implement bilingual education at various school levels, and be aware of the potential for ameliorating existing unequal socio-political relationships between linguistic varieties in Taiwan.

Multiculturalism

Multiculturalism has generated much interest in western countries, e.g. the United States, Australia, and Canada to name a few, but it also resonates with the diverse cultural and linguistic situation in Taiwan. Recognition of linguistic varieties, protection of minority rights and adherence to international law are three major concerns for all multiculturalists (Hornberger 1998; Koenig 1999; May 1998, 2000; Smith 1998; Sue 1997; Taylor 1992). According to Koenig (1999), the dynamics of the modern nation-state have had a double effect on linguistic minority groups. On the downside, the (re-)ethnicization of language in the ethnic model of the nation-state and the general ideal of national monolingualism itself has discriminated against non-dominant linguistic groups. More positively, the successive establishment of a legal system based on the recognition of individual rights and growing support for a de-ethnicized understanding of language has highlighted the illegitimacy of discriminating against minorities on language grounds and has provided linguistic minorities with the resources to claim legal and political recognition (p. 62). In the wake of increasing demands from minority groups for rights and recognition, the multicultural language policies are most likely to succeed in the double task of respecting particular identities and maintaining social integration in a shared public sphere (ibid, p. 58).

From a multiculturalist perspective, language policy can serve as a strategy not only to gain overdue recognition of the rights of minority groups and protect them from discrimination but also to provide choices for what language a child is to be educated in. This approach differs from the assimilation and differentiation approaches where languages other than the dominant one are marginalized, and where speakers of such languages are discriminated against for speaking and acting differently and their futures jeopardized. However, even when the state intervenes to help minorities, as for example by providing educational and professional advancement incentives and protections through legislation such as Taiwan's draft "language equality law" (*yuyan pingdengfa*), speakers of minority languages such as Hakka, Tai-yu and the island's aboriginal languages still face an uphill battle dealing with various sets of dilemmas. For example, interest groups may want to elevate the status of, and secure funding for, linguistic varieties such as Hakka, Tai-yu, and aboriginal languages, while finding themselves at odds over which local variety should be chosen for (written) representation. Without standardization and representation, these varieties are best treated as dialects, not really considered as serious contenders for status promotion and education advancement. In fact, scholars such as Chang (2002) have discussed the social conditions, challenges and transformations Taiwan has undergone by recognizing minority rights and trying to reconcile diversity in the face of mounting pressure for democratization. In the language equality law, drafted by a group of concerned scholars, linguistic diversity is not endorsed as such but is encouraged as a right of protection from discrimination and as mother tongue education. Elsewhere, serious debates on how to best handle issues of language diversity, language vitality and national progress in a multicultural context have sparked intense discussions among scholars and administrators. The 2005 series of conferences on language policy perspectives in a multicultural context hosted by the Linguistic Institute at Academia Sinica is an effective case in point. There, Hakka, Tai-yu, and aboriginal representatives and scholars engaged in discussions of issues such as minority rights, bilingual education and language policy in a multicultural context.

Indigenous Language Rights

In Taiwan, indigenous language education is at the forefront of the "language policy in a multicultural context" debate not only because the Mandarin-only policy once practiced by the KMT subjected the speaking of indigenous languages to discrimination and marginalization but also because the revising of their status and functions will be seen as a test of true multicultural language policy.

Steven May (2000) points out that debates on minority rights address complexities of the language-identity link, the controversies surrounding group-based rights, and the often-leveled charge of cultural relativism. At the same time, the debates highlight hegemonies implicit (and, at times, explicit) in the traditional (linguistic) organization of nation-states. The challenge, therefore, is to rethink nation-states and the national identities therein, in ways more plural and inclusive (p. 380). Moreover, only by a greater recognition of minority language rights can the prospect of the more representational multinational and multilingual state be secured (ibid, p. 381).

On the domestic front, independent-minded scholars such as Shih (2001, 2004) have advocated the rights of minorities, attacking the Han-centered ideology of Chinese nationalism and monolithic language policy-making. Other scholars have been more concerned about whether debates on amendments for minority rights will adhere to international laws on human rights and collective identity. For example, Simon (2005) points to Taiwan's deepened democratization and the nation's acceptance of evolving international standards in human rights, including the demands of indigenous peoples as expressed in such documents as the UN High Commission for Human Rights' 1994 Draft Declaration on Indigenous Rights (UNHCHR 1994),[2] the International Labor Organization Convention 169 (ILO 1989)[3] and Agenda 21 of the UN Conference on Environment and Development. Proposed amendments to Taiwan's constitution would include collective rights for indigenous peoples, making Taiwan one of the most progressive countries in the world in that respect (ibid, pp. 2-3).

Representation for minorities has also been put on the political front burner. For example, the Council of Indigenous Peoples (CIP) was set up in 1996, marking a breakthrough in the Republic of China's nationality policy. Since then the formulation of Indigenous policies has been placed in the hands of the Indigenous groups, and all Indigenous affairs have been brought under the jurisdiction of this specific ministerial-level agency.[4] In May 4, 2001, the Legislative Yuan passed "The Council for Hakka Affairs Organization Law (CHA)."[5] The CHA Council began operating on June 14 of that year. In its political makeup, it is exercising the powers of both people and the government to shoulder responsibility for perpetuating the life of minority languages and culture. It is fighting for the Hakka's rights and future, and ultimately aims to advance Taiwan to a modern society that respects all racial and ethnic groups.

Bilingual Education

We look at bilingual education in terms of how forces such as globalization and indigenization come into play, generating dilemmas in language policy. The importance of English has been linked with professionalism, modernization and internationalization, while the stress on local language teaching is identified with culture, tradition, and authenticity. With enthusiasm increasing to participate in a more globalized community, the MOE has been motivated to change the onset of English language instruction from the fifth grade to the third grade. Meanwhile, the MOE mandated the teaching of local languages as a formal school subject in response to rising ethnolinguistic awareness, starting in the fall semester of 2001. Pupils were to receive local language education from the first to the sixth grades by choosing between Hakka, Tai-yu, or one of the aboriginal languages. According to Tse (2001), the goals for local language education were competence in basic listening comprehension, the ability to use transcription symbols as an aid to pronunciation, and simple oral proficiency (p. 8). Pupils were to be exposed to the sense and sound of the local language and were to learn to appreciate and respect cultural and linguistic diversity.

English, in contrast, has been treated with more than aesthetic appreciation. With the U.S. and the UK exercising the strongest Western influence on Taiwan in terms of technology exports, and with popular culture affecting the daily lives of the island's people, local interest in acquiring English proficiency has become intense. Sectors other than educational establishments are becoming involved; for example, employers are asking perspective employees to provide credentials of adequate English proficiency. As a result, there has been a surge in support for taking national and/or international certified English proficiency examinations such as the GEPT (General English Proficiency Test) and the TOEIC (Test of English for International Communication), and consequently, an increasing number of cram schools have been set up to meet the demand for training.

Apart from practical concerns, the unrelenting interest in acquiring English proficiency has a socio-political dimension. People in Taiwan see themselves in an international setting, but in addition, opting for English in place of Mandarin or other linguistic varieties such as Hakka, Tai-yu, or the aboriginal languages is a deliberate way to avoid another ethnolinguistic conflict, the one in which Mandarin is identified with the political regime in Beijing, Tai-yu with independence, and Hakka or aboriginal tongues with separatism (cf. Tse 2000, p.161). In this respect, English with its economic and technological clout further serves as a "neutral" medium for inter-ethnic communication as well as international communication.

In the literature of sociolinguistics, we find ample examples of former colonies of super powers opting for a non-ethnic related language to appease tensions, competition and conflict. Such a choice might also be pragmatically motivated, for English is seen not only as an international language but also as a language of technological and business might. For example, according to Bokhorst-Heng (1998), bilingual education in Singapore is premised on the role of English meeting the pragmatic needs of the nation (globalization, economic progress and technological progress, as well as inter-ethnic communication), while the mother-tongue languages of Mandarin, Malay, and Tamil are seen as meeting the country's cultural needs (ibid, p. 44). The Singaporean case might serve as a point of reference, but there is some discrepancy between Taiwan and Singapore. Each, it is true, has been influenced more if not less by Chinese culture and language and has been trying to come up with ingenuous ways to maintain economic and national stability in the midst of ethno-linguistic tensions. As in Singapore, English language education in Taiwan has been stressed for its practicality, international status and economic clout. However, unlike Singapore, increasingly democratized Taiwan does not associate English with lower standards of morality or with decadence, especially compared with the influence of Chinese.

The current language situation in Taiwan education reflects the beginning of the government's acknowledgement of previously denied rights of minority groups and the elevation of their languages from marginalized status. The symbolic implications are national as well as transnational: such multilingual choices represent statements about a nation's past and future and its relations to other political bodies. Implied as well in Taiwan's case are statements about its historical ties to China and contention among its ethnic groups. Beyond the implied need for a balancing act between globalization and indigenization on the one hand and national cohesion and linguistic diversity on the other, unequal power relations among different speakers must be addressed. Especially, English education in Taiwan must not be treated obsessively or in a paranoid fashion, with English proficiency seen as a panacea for educational and professional incompetence. A disproportionate amount of time, energy and resources have already been poured into metropolitan areas, where children start learning English before they acquire a firm base in their mother tongues. As Price (2005) rightly points out, some observers have even begun to worry that ethnic equality is a social impossibility as long as economic advantage remains predicated on English language ability (p. 1).

In fact, English, too, is being blamed today for suppressing language diversity and marginalizing other tongues,[6] a problem most often associated with Mandarin during the KMT heyday when hegemonic and exclusive ethno-linguistic monolingualism was deliberately practiced. Obviously, how language diversities were viewed by the authorities in the KMT era was very different from how they are viewed now. To get a broader perspective on the management of language diversity over time, we will now take a historical journey to see how things have evolved.

Socio-historical Review of Language Policy in Taiwan

Having touched on crucial issues in language choices associated with multiculturalism, we turn to the evolution of language policy, or as some would have it to the lack of clear evolution, since the Dutch (1624-1662) and Spanish (1626-1642) colonizations, the Qing Dynasty era in Taiwan (1683-1895), the Japanese era (1895-1945) and the KMT era (1945-2000). To ease comparison of policies from different administrations we offer our analysis from three perspectives—socio-structural (the macro-political), epistemological, and strategic.

Taiwan for the European powers in the seventeenth century was another port to be conquered in Southeast Asia to satisfy their insatiable appetite for raw materials and to further European maritime military expansion. As Heylen (2001) explains, the Chinese had first tried to set up settlements in various locations alongside the aboriginal lowlanders. The majority of these Chinese settlers were fishermen, traders, or pirates, who raided the Chinese coastal areas or engaged in trade with their Japanese counterparts (p. 202). The rough sea made it difficult to approach the island, and the practices of headhunting tribes further made it a literal killing field. Some of the aboriginal tribes displayed the characteristics of subsistence communities or "primitive" societies: that is, they were pre-literate, with no open market and a simple division of labor based on age and sex. Religion was not separated from socio-cultural life. Shamanesses presided over a narrow but rigorously controlled morality; backed by tradition, sorcery and witchcraft, they regulated the lives of the people (Heylen 2001, p. 205). Under these dire circumstances, the European powers intervened not only to trade with the natives in competition with the Chinese and Japanese but also to civilize barbarians.

The lack of a lingua franca on the island, a laissez-faire policy by the Qing Chinese government and an absence of writing systems among the natives made it relatively easy for missionaries to introduce Christianity. The introduction of the Roman alphabet was more than just a tool of conversion for the Dutch Reformed Church. An imported language classification and the establishment of the SinKan tongue as the official vernacular for an area and its surroundings were more, too, than language engineering; it was also defiance of the Spanish Roman Catholic prescription of Latin. Thus, the choice of a native language can be seen as a continuation of religious antagonism between the Protestant tradition, which advocated proselytizing in the vernacular or the daily speech of the people, and Roman Catholicism, which considered Latin and the Bible as the orthodox medium for religion and civilization.

The Dutch missionaries' insistence on using local languages for instruction and evangelization proved greatly successful. Local languages were categorized, grammatical rules were formulated and Christian doctrines were translated into the local tongues. Today, some scholars view the introduction of the Roman alphabet to transcribe the aboriginal languages and Tai-yu and its applications in transcribing the Bible as proof of the languages' long written history as well as their much older oral form (Kloeter 2005). The distinctive writing forms and history further support claims that these linguistic varieties shouldn't be seen as mere local dialects lacking writing and grammar systems or as subordinate varieties of Chinese (Hong 1988). However, at the time, authorities only tolerated local languages insofar as they helped propagate Christianity and serve the needs of territorial conquest and further colonization of the island. In other words, the embracing of local languages had to be done in the interest of promoting social stability. In fact, the Dutch administration had shifted its focus to securing new footholds among the natives, while organizing and exercising control over the Chinese settlers (cf. Heylen 2001, pp. 214-15). During the latter half of Dutch rule (1642-62), attempts were made to introduce Dutch as the lingua franca. Linguistically speaking, Dutch colonization introduced the Roman alphabet to the natives and set up a European language classification system. These were used to classify local languages, to transcribe the Bible and to catechize as well as for practical purposes such as documenting transactions.

Socio-politically, the situation prevailing in Taiwan during Dutch colonization was similar to what Errington (2001) describes as an exercise of linguistic territoriality by European powers. He states that colonial states and missionary jurisdictions shared a territorial logic that was similarly inscribed in colonial linguistic works, presupposing mappings of monolithic language within demarcated boundaries. Within these bounded confines, ethnolinguistically homogeneous groups were conceived as localized and naturalized "tribes" or "ethnicities" (p. 24). Assumptions about the naturalness of monoglot conditions furthered for the Europeans a strategic purpose of managing language diversity in the locale. Historiographies by missionaries show how the linguistic descriptions they authored, augmented by print literacy, served as a means for powerfully yet intimately conceptualizing, inscribing, and interacting with colonialized peoples on terms not of the their own choosing (ibid).

The Qing administration that followed the Dutch and Spanish administrations adopted a center/periphery mentality in ruling Taiwan. According to Friedman (2005), the Qing intervened educationally in Taiwan during their rule over the island in two major ways, by introducing examination quotas for the most loyal, and by adopting a curriculum modeled on Confucianism. This not only helped the state control local prefectures but also had a great impact on ethnic relations, especially among minorities such as the Hakka and the aborigines, who benefited the most from such policies (cf. p. 87). Regional examination quotas were an important means of social control, often utilized by the Qing to reward loyal supporters, ensure that power would be evenly distributed geographically, and to encourage the development of local elites "to cultivate the growth of a Confucian literati in regions where the state's influence was weak" (ibid; also in Shepherd, 1993, p. 210).

The curriculum of these aborigine schools was modeled directly on that of the community schools in the villages: "Emphasis was at first on character recognition and calligraphy and then on recitation and memorization of the [classical Chinese] texts. But the main focus was on Confucian morality" (ibid, p. 88; also in Shepherd 1993, p. 372). The medium of instruction more often than not was one of the locally spoken Chinese dialects (Southern Min or Hakka) rather than Mandarin. The native aboriginal languages were not taught, while sinicization was encouraged (Tse 2000, p.155).

Strategically, the Qing administration's emphasis on Confucian ethics in its intervention in the education of the locals in Taiwan shared similar practical motives with those of the Dutch—to "civilize" the locals—but, as Friedman (2005) rightly pointed out, the Qing were not as enthusiastic nor as willing to appropriate as many resources for the "uncivilized," while tensions among the locals served a strategic purpose for the Qing, that of divide and rule (cf. 2005, p. 91).

Summing up, the Dutch and Spanish colonial periods brought waves of missionaries to the island. With them, various community schools were set up and the Roman alphabet was introduced for religious and pragmatic functions. The choice and use of local tongues, Latin, or Dutch for administration and communication was the result of intense power struggles among the administrators, missionaries and locals. At times, the missionaries' zeal to evangelize the locals was in step with the Dutch authorities' interest in trade. At other times, these two group interests clashed. European epistemology looked at Taiwan's linguistic diversity, classified the local languages, and exercised great tolerance so long as social stability was maintained and daily transactions were carried out smoothly.

The laissez-faire attitude of the authorities took one drastic turn after 1895 with the Japanese colonization and another after 1945 when the KMT occupied Taiwan at the close of the Second World War and later retreated there en masse from the mainland after losing the Chinese civil war. Each occupier adopted a nation-state model and introduced new ideologies to the language policy scene. Nationalism ran high during both occupations, especially when Japan became engaged in the Second World War and the KMT found itself facing the Chinese Communists as their sworn enemies. In both cases language policy was part of nation building policy, crucial to the engineering of a unified nation and an imagined civilization during a state of emergency and imminent danger, with threats from a military enemy to be combated and ethnic conflicts among the natives to be appeased. The nation-state ideologies that were applied envisioned a homogenous nation and a harmonious state where the people should be satisfied with using one common language.

According to Steven May (2000), an emphasis on cultural and linguistic homogeneity associated with the rise of political nationalism is predicated on the notion of "nation-state congruence." It holds that the boundaries of political and national identity should coincide. In this view, people who are citizens of a particular state should also, ideally, be members of the same national collective (p. 370). The inevitable consequence of such a political imperative is the establishment of an ethnically exclusive and culturally and linguistically homogeneous nation-state, a realm from which minority languages and cultures are effectively banished. Indeed, this is the "ideal" model to which most nation-states (and nationalist movements) still aspire, albeit in the face of a far more complex (contested) multiethnic and multi-linguistic reality (ibid).

Socio-politically, May's insights on the implementation of nation-state ideology and its consequences speak volumes for the situation in Taiwan, which not only fits the circumstances where such ideology arises but also has suffered the consequences of one-nation, one-language monolingualism hegemony. Both the Japanese and the KMT administrations adopted stringent assimilation policies where the natives and their local tongues were subjected to power ideologies such as Japanese/Chinese civilization, nationalism and patriotism. Ironically, the nationalistic ideology is reluctant to relinquish its reign even after the demise of the colonial master. The people of Taiwan saw this before as the KMT replaced Japanese with the Chinese language and a China-centered ideology, and they are seeing it again as some of the Taiwan-independence advocates, riding on the high tide of democracy, try to replace Chinese and all things Chinese with Tai-yu and a de-Chinaization ideology.

The Japanese assimilatory language policies consisted of three stages: pacification, assimilation and, especially after 1941, complete Japanization. According to Lai, Myers and Wei (1991), in April 1941, the Taiwan governor-general's office launched a total mobilization campaign to transform all Taiwanese into imperial subjects (pp. 29-30). These stages not only coincided with Tokyo's military expansion but also helped execute imperial Japan's national imagination as the Greater East Asia Co-prosperity Sphere (*Dadongya Gongrongquan*). Chinese varieties were first tolerated, banned later and completely banished eventually from all public domains. Public servants were even required to use Japanese in all public and private domains (Chen 1996; Huang 1993). The repressive and discriminatory practice of these policies relegated speakers of Chinese dialects and aboriginal languages to the status of second-class citizens in Taiwan (cf. Tse 2000, p.155).

The KMT regime brought another wave of monolingual policy to the island. With the Communist threat looming, the KMT had to engineer ways to legitimize its rule over Taiwan as a base to recapture the mainland, eradicate a half-century-long Japanese colonial influence, and resolve ethnic tensions and contentions. In fact, it was under these extraneous circumstances that the KMT promoted a standardized Mandarin,[7] emphasized the homogeneity of a Chinese ethnicity, and advocated the quintessential nature of Chinese culture as major instruments to lend legitimacy to its rule, achieve national unity and symbolically upstage the Chinese Communists. Under the nation-state model, language, culture and the state were all one. Heller (1999) provides an interesting parallel from the French Canadian scene, pointing out that nationalistic ideologies focus on authenticity and integrity. Language is the inherent, essential property of the people and the guarantor of peoplehood. Properties of the language, its correctness, its beauty, and so on make it uniquely valuable and important as the symbol and vehicle of public life (p. 339).

While the Communists on the mainland opted for simplified characters, Putonghua, and Hanyu Pinyin as their continuation of the language movement, the KMT tried to upstage its counterpart by imagining itself as the state (Republic of China) and as the Chinese nation, composed of a homogenous Chinese culture in which all ethnic groups spoke a common language, Mandarin Chinese. According to Hsiao (1990) the enactment of the nation-state model was seen as a solution to the problem of political unity that culminated in the KMT's "Chinaization" endeavor (p. 312). The usage of Mandarin as a national language became a testament to the Chineseness of the KMT state. Hence speakers of non-

Mandarin languages were asked to abolish their "localism" by "sacrificing dialects" (p. 307).

As part of its effort to reintegrate Taiwan into the Chinese fold, the KMT enforced a strict policy that entailed using only Mandarin for official affairs, in schools, on radio, and on television.

> Television was first aired [in Taiwan] and Taiwanese shows were most popular, which caused some jealousy. So in 1972 the government ordered that all television stations could not air more than one hour per day of Taiwanese-language programs and that hour had to be broken up into two segments at lunch and at night. During the 6:30 p.m. prime-time hour, only one of the three stations could air a Taiwanese language program. In 1976, another rule was passed which said that all television shows had to be in Mandarin and the shows in Taiwanese would be gradually phased out over the year. (Wachman 1994, p. 107) (quoted from Lin Yu-ti, *Tai-wan chiao-yu mien-mu 40 nien*, [Faces of Taiwan's Education Over 40 Years].(Taipei: Cultural Division of *Tzu-li Wan-pao* [Independence Evening Post], 1987, p. 114.

Tse (2000) stated the three stages of the KMT language policy: 1) transition (1945-1969), which emphasized the eradication of all Japanese influence upon the general population in all aspects of life, and discouragement of the use of dialects in pubic domains; 2) solidification of Mandarin as the national language (1970-1986), during which linguistic varieties other than Mandarin faced more stringent treatment; and finally, after the 1987 repeal of martial law, a gradual trend toward multilingualism, during which policies calling for mother tongue education, bilingual education and the preservation of endangered varieties of aboriginal language were designed and implemented (cf. pp. 156-57).

Summing up, the twice over monolingualism enforced under the auspices of the Japanese regime and the KMT regime nation-states was born of extraneous socio-political circumstances where the authorities were variously engaged in international military exercises or threatened by civil war as well as by ethnic discontent. Strategically, a high-handed nationalism was called for in order to imagine the state as consisting of one homogeneous nation within which all spoke the common language. Language, or better yet the designated standard language, was a powerful symbol charged with nationalistic ideologies such as patriotism, and twice-over monolingualism drastically changed the function and status of minority languages. The imposition of Japanese gradually decreased the functions of local languages and the number of their speakers, eventually replacing them as a new generation grew up identifying with the Japanese culture, language and state. The KMT's policy produced similar effects, with standard Mandarin as the enforced language for Chinese people. Mandarin was imposed to replace Japanese in all public and private functions. Language diversity was discouraged and eventually banned. A new generation was raised where Mandarin was used not only as the lingua franca among ethnic groups in Taiwan but also in private domains such as communications with parents and grandparents.

The Changing Tide: From Imagined Community to Imagined Divisions

Having set out the socio-historical contexts of how language diversities in Taiwan have been viewed by different administrations, we return to the "post-nationalistic" scene of democratization, challenges to the old power structure that was based on a Chinese and China dominated ideology, and the recalibration and reinterpretation of political symbols such as language diversity to accommodate pluralism. The KMT, which initiated policy changes and political reforms either voluntarily or under pressure from public opinion, belatedly saw what resistance to changes and reforms were doing to the party and its fortunes. Rival parties were legitimized, among the most influential the Democratic Progressive Party (DPP), which adopted a platform of independence and advocated a quintessential Taiwanese identity aimed at abolishing all things Chinese. The DPP emerged as a serious player in the 1980s, contended for domination in the 1990s, and became the ruling party in the year 2000. All aspects of cultural, national and language policies and practices became the objects of renewed contention. This time, the government was forced to reinvent Taiwan according to a democratized, multicultural blueprint.

Among the most vocal groups were the independence-minded who, like their KMT counterparts, saw language as an indispensable part of culture and nationhood and who advocated the right to be educated in one's mother tongue, a separate writing system, and an eventual break-away from the Chinese-centered ideology practiced by the KMT. Such ideology sounds strangely familiar to that proposed by the KMT at the time of their take-over of Taiwan in the 1940s. For example, Cheng (1993) stated that "only when we write Tai-yu that we can think [in] Tai-yu and that we can appreciate native authenticity and reality" (p. 186). Hsiau (1997) further pointed out that for advocates of the Tai-yu writing system, to abolish Chinese characters as an inept instrument to voice Taiwaneseness was to slough off Chineseness; to have a Tai-yu writing system was to recognize the existence of a distinctive cultural tradition. Such a view suggests the development of a new national identity, one challenging the KMT's "Chinaization" of the island (p. 312).

Like the Mandarin-only movement, proponents of the Tai-yu movement, by adopting as their platform an anti-Mandarin-only and anti-Chinese center policy, also faced counter forces from other interest groups such as those representing Hakka and aboriginal speakers. Among these, the most impressive was the "Return of my Mother Tongue" movement in 1988, organized and staged mostly by the Hakka as an effective attack on Tai-yu's claim to language and representation totality. As a result of these polyphonic movements, restrictions on dialect broadcasts were loosened, representation for minority language groups was established, and dialect instruction was included in the school curriculum.

The Dilemma of Mandarin Only or Mandarin Plus Language Education

Contention over resources and representation among Mandarin, Tai-yu, Hakka, and aboriginal groups can be seen as part of the growing pain of a democratizing socio-political context where no group could retain a monopoly of power. In such a heated situation, equality and rights were prevailing themes. Various political representations were made; among the most vocal were efforts by the Hakka, Tai-yu, and aboriginal groups to advance the distinctiveness of their history, language and rights in order to secure resources and representation in education and politics. Moreover, whether Mandarin should still retain official status in a democratizing Taiwan also became a matter of debate. As mentioned before, much of the contention surrounding this issue derives from the historical legacy of twice-over monolingualism in Taiwan dating from the Japanese colonization (1895-1945) and KMT administration (1945-2000), when nonindigenous languages—Japanese in the first instance and Mandarin in the second—were set up as the national language while languages spoken by the majority were marginalized and subordinated. Japanese, after English, is still among one of the most popular foreign languages, and some survivors of the generation that experienced Japanese occupation still enjoy using Japanese. Mandarin, meanwhile, is still in demand as the symbolic language of business and politics after half a century of Mandarin-only language in education. With the increasing trade dependence throughout transnational Chinese communities, Mandarin still enjoys default official status even in the face of challenges from radicals who view it as "Beijing dialect," thus not suitable for official status. A generation of Taiwanese has grown up using Mandarin in public and among family members in private domains. To them, the use of other Chinese varieties such as Hakka and Tai-yu is non-pragmatic and offers little value other than that of fostering ethnic solidarity.

Thus, the Mandarin-only assimilationist language policy has remained the default policy, and its unassailable stature is further assured by waves of globalization, where economic advancement and competitiveness are high on the educational and political agenda. On the other hand, increasing democratization has awakened ethnic consciousness among Hakka, Tai-yu-speaking, and aboriginal groups who see Taiwan as multilingual and multicultural and demand that ethnic diversity should not only be protected, but also actively promoted. The efforts of these groups to advance their rights and strengthen their legal framework so far have only produced "tolerance rights"[8] in which their usage of varieties of Chinese or aboriginal languages is safe from discrimination. Whether and when "promotion" rights can be granted, i.e., bilingualism or multilingualism can be institutionalized at different levels in education and in public domains, has not been decided. The views of assimilationists and pluralists on national unity, economic equality and rights are in constant disagreement and, in this, we find parallels in the English-only and English-plus movements in the U.S., parallels that offer us an even broader perspective.

We can learn several lessons from the English-only assimilationist and the English-plus pluralist debates in the U.S. The English-only faction sees using English and providing transitional-only bilingual programs as a way to elevate minorities from their subordinate socio-political status. Further, the use and implementation of non-English in public domains under the auspices of the state, and the appropriation of public funding for such programs, is seen as a political ploy conducive to competition, corruption and animosity among different constituents. Various minorities, it is argued, will be manipulated to believe that they are victims and thus stirred to a state of constant contention with other minority constituents and with an English-speaking population bent on protecting the status quo. In contrast, the pluralists advocate indefinitely-extended bilingual programs. They see the U.S. as quintessentially multilingual and multicultural and believe that genuine equality can only be achieved by recognizing that fact and by tendering to individuals their language rights even at state expenditure. A good question posed by Ronald Schmidt (2000) might serve as a summary of the crux of the contending views on equality. In pursuing equality, where do we draw the line between language groups that deserve state promotion and those that do not? If there is no line, then equality, for assimilationists, can mean that all individuals should have an equal opportunity to realize their dreams in the U.S. to the best of their ability in the language of their ancestors (cf. ibid, p. 158).

In terms of rights for non-English language implementation and representation, many pluralists believe that equal democratic rights for language minorities requires the promotion of minority languages through public policies that employ the power of the state to help maintain and develop minority languages and cultures. Assimilationists, on the other hand, would restrict to the private sector both the terrain of, and support for, any language rights of non-English speakers. Governments, in their view, have no legitimate reason to recognize or promote non-English languages in U.S. society (ibid, p. 160). In fact, the situation of the U.S. may be quite complex. Our comparison is just a generalized overview and it is advisable for concerned readers to appreciate that, although no trace of English as the language of government is found in the American Constitution, there are individual states that back English and record it in their constitution as their sole official language.

The conflicting views over equality and rights between the assimilationists and pluralists are born not just of different political beliefs but also derive from how national identity is perceived. Is the U.S. by default a monolingual society which people should be satisfied with as one national unit, a unit where one dominant language assures the status quo but also redeems aspiring minorities in transition to socio-political upward mobility? An alternative view is that the U.S.

is composed of people who speak in different tongues, that people who have not mastered English suffer from economic, social and political subordination, and that their deemed equality in society and their right to use a language other than English should be endorsed by the state. The national identity issues are deeply resonant for an emerging democracy such as Taiwan, which has undergone drastic transformations in its search for an identity amidst domestic and international political upheavals.

Contentions and Predicaments for a Multicultural Taiwan

Socio-politically, the challenges to the Mandarin-only language policy and a Chinese centered national policy have been born largely out of discontent with repressive monolingualism and mono-culturalism, as well as out of the considerable liberation that has accompanied increasing democratization since the 1980s. Some even argue that the challenges and associated sympathies were on the political agenda even before the lifting of martial law in 1987. For example, Allen Chun (2002b) states that political transformation and discursive mutation had long taken place within the KMT regime. They were evident in the late 1970s when discussions of the predicament of subordinating ethnic and linguistic differences within a China centered civilization surfaced, and the legitimacy of subjecting Taiwanese to the rule of "outsider" ethnic Chinese was challenged. Strategically, as argued by Chun, such "multiculturalism" was a facet of the broader Taiwan political indigenization that directly followed the country's expulsion from the United Nations, and reflected also a policy to promote market liberalization in the global economy (cf. Chun 2002b, pp. 2-3).

In addition to the personal role of strong-minded politicians and discursive political maneuverings in effecting change, some of the most influential movers and shakers have been driven by the idea of emphasizing the diversity of historical experience and linguistic vitality. For example, an ex-minister of the MOE, Kuo Wei-fan, proposed in 1994 the idea of concentric circles *(tongxinyuan)* in one's identity development. This idea reflected a three-step plan to expose Taiwanese youth to outside reality by letting them "stand on Taiwan, have consideration for China, and open their eyes to the world" (cf. Corcuff 2002, p. 87). On a similar note, and in terms of national identity formation, the ex-president Lee Teng-hui, while campaigning for Ma Ying-jeou in the 1998 Taipei mayoral race, used a non-ethnolingual centered way of consolidating a national, international and even cultural ethos. He used a term he had coined, "New Taiwanese," to include those who identified with Taiwan regardless of personal ethnicity, language or nationality.

The political plurality emphasized by Lee served several strategic purposes. Friedman (2005) noted that Lee Teng-hui strategically adopted a multiculturalism ideology that effectively undermined efforts to promote Taiwanese nationalism by doing three things. First, it served to de-legitimize a vision of Taiwanese nationalism grounded in Hoklo culture, by placing on equal grounds the cultural traditions of Taiwan's Hakkas, Mainlanders, and aborigines. Secondly, it avoided a wholesale rejection of Chinese nationalism by viewing culture as a series of concentric circles, radiating outward from individual communities to the entire Taiwanese nation but also beyond to include the greater Chinese cultural sphere and global culture as well. This ideology, it should be noted, further served to enhance the power of the native elite within the KMT, protecting them from loss of power to those outside the party (cf. p. 27).

On the language policy front, the implementation of a new course, "Taiwanese Native Languages," in the grades 1-9 curriculum was another move away from China/Taiwan centered nationalism. The new curriculum got under way in 2001; it defined native languages as Tai-yu, Hakka or one of the aboriginal languages, and required students to take one hour of these subjects per week. Meanwhile, the teaching of Mandarin remained impeded. English, introduced in the fifth grade in 2001, was moved up to the third grade in 2003 (cf. Yeh et. al 2004). Friedman (2005) rightly points out that the new curriculum marked the emergence of a new and uniquely Taiwanese conception of nationhood, one that departs from the monolithic cultural nationalism of the Japanese and Chinese eras. This can be seen in the fact that Tai-yu did not simply replace Japanese and Mandarin as the new "national language." To be sure, there are those who desire to make Tai-yu the new National Language, but what is surprising is that Taiwan has instead replaced cultural nationalism with multiculturalism (p. 4).

Summing up, the evolution of a pluralistic language policy in multicultural Taiwan was born out of a series of socio-political events which movers and shakers exploited to seize the moment and challenge the essentializing nature of a Chinese centered national policy and a monopolizing Mandarin-only language policy. Unlike Quebec, where the acceptance of French signified negation of an essentializing English-centered cultural and national policy and a recognition of the contribution and equality of the French native/immigrant cultures and languages, Taiwan has had an additional political agenda to consider—how to counter its increasing isolation from the international political scene due to an ambiguous political state.[9] The recognition of cultural and linguistic groups other than Chinese has thus been a necessary political step to diversify Taiwan in order to differentiate it from mainland China, to shun the suicidal politics of independence-minded Taiwanese radicals, and to stay in synch with global laws protecting minority rights and equality. A revised language policy for education has tried to move away from the "imagined community" of either a Republic of China (ROC) state premised on a China-center ideology and Mandarin-only political symbolism, or a Taiwan independent state favored by DPP radicals where Taiwanese essentialism is privileged. It has tried to move instead to a multicultural state where "imagined divisions" advocated by political constituents have been successful in pushing for a legal framework and rights for mother tongue education. A language policy born out of these circumstances not only emphasizes the strength and contributions of mother tongue languages and bilingual education but also stresses the importance of English and Japanese to a lesser extent as they relate to technology and international trade.

Multiculturalism with Hindsight

We are left wondering whether institutionalized multiculturalism modeled after countries such as Canada can truly be implemented in Taiwan. In Canada, there is indeed a policy of multiculturalism, though it is more politically oriented in the sense that only English-French bilingualism is actually promoted and applied. In the Canadian context, multiculturalism means that the cultures and the languages of all immigrants are to be respected; better still, tolerated. True, one of the hidden aims of the official bilingual policy is to assimilate minority languages, especially those of immigrants, and to homogenize the country's linguistic landscape. However, it is noteworthy that the Canadian government does not take any steps against a community that endeavors to revitalize a language. In contrast, as we learned from Taiwan history in the second section, although the island has always been inhabited by people speaking different tongues and practicing distinct cultures, attempts were made to mold a single culture and language as byproducts of strong nationalism practiced by the Japanese and KMT administrations during their days in the red and the blue/white suns. Much of that has been challenged and changed. The turn of the twenty-first century has brought a new curriculum where Mandarin along with Hakka, Tai-yu, and aboriginal languages are included. Tolerance is practiced and rights are exercised to ensure that individuals will not be discriminated against for speaking languages other than Mandarin. Legal frameworks and improved representation have been established. Yet such "equality" and "rights" are perhaps just initial steps toward a genuine multiculturalism, since Mandarin and English still enjoy unflagging support among most parents and children. In language instruction an unequal distribution between the haves and have-nots is most obvious in the countryside, where lack of materials and qualified teachers is most severe. Economic rationalism has been one of the major reasons for the renewed importance of Mandarin and English. Apart from economics and pragmatism, language rights issues tend to be used to mobilize voters and thus can be seen as proxy wars in power struggles between the KMT and the DPP in the first place and among other constituents to a lesser extent. In the current situation, we are facing a liberalized language policy in which forums are provided for different voices. The new language policies in education can only be seen as initial steps toward a genuine multiculturalism in which a mature political structure institutionalizing "equality" and preventing "domination" will assure multiculturalism's equal development.

With insights from the debates over English-only and English-plus in the U.S. and Canada's experience with multiculturalism and bilingual education, we are able to see alternatives to a stringent monolingual policy bound with national identity. Moreover, we can see from history that twice over monolingualism is very much a "modern" product of strong nationalism practiced by first the Japanese and then the KMT regime. Whether a language should still be conceptualized as an ideological national symbol and all the others seen as threats is surely doubtful. The notion certainly runs against the trend of multiculturalism where the state simply tries to set up fair conditions for all languages in order to ensure rights and equality for all. In such a context, languages can indeed be seen as mere practical instruments and the effectiveness of any language as a tool can be determined by those individuals or groups using the tool.

In the concluding chapter, we will not only sum up the major findings of each chapter but also try to use them to build a possible model for the interactions among the transnational Chinese communities. We argue that whether the evolved Taiwan consciousness is Japanese, Chinese, or Taiwanese, it is today of the most ethnocentric form, a product of nationalistic discourse. Taking a monolithic view of either language or identity is passé seen from a "post-modern," democratizing context. We will argue for a more pluralistic view of language and identity in which the competition between local and national identities, special interest allegiances and personal advancement all play a role in the Taiwan post-modern and multicultural context. This can be achieved by first proposing a hybrid Chinese where a poly-center norm is not attached to single political center with an intrinsic link to identity, and then by proposing a marginal concentric idea of identity.

Notes

1. According to *Language Loyalties: A Source Book on the Official English Controversy*, ed. James Crawford (University of Chicago Press, 1992), the U.S. Constitution is silent on the issue of an official language, although as late as 1987, two-thirds of Americans who responded to a national survey believed that English was the official language of the United States.

2. For more details on the Draft United Nations Declaration on the Rights of Indigenous Peoples, Geneva, UNHCHR, please access:
http://www.unhchr.ch/huridocda/hurdoca.nsf.

3. For more details on ILO C169 *Indigenous and Tribal Peoples Convention*, Geneva: ILO, please access http://www.ilo.org/ilolex/english/convdisp1.htm

4. For more details on the CIP, please refer to http://www.apc.gov.tw

5. For more details on the CHA, please refer to http://www.hakka.gov.tw

6. There are concerned scholars who oppose the argument that English can be viewed as utilitarian, i.e. simply a public good that permits progress. For detailed discussion on this point, please refer to Wright 2004, pp. 165-172.

7. According to Chen Ping (2001), the KMT regime at first practiced a different kind of national language movement when it controlled the mainland. When Guoyu (the national language) was first promoted as the standard spoken language there, it was not intended to replace local dialects for informal use. The goal was a bilingual society in

which people acquired proficiency in Guoyu and in their native dialect. However, intense ethnic tensions in the Chinese world as well as military conflict with the Chinese Communists prompted the KMT to switch eventually to an essentially monolingual policy, with Guoyu serving as the sole legitimate language in schools and with the expectation that it would replace local dialects for all occasions in due course (cf. p. 104).

8. According to Ronald Schmidt, Sr. (2000), the debate over toleration-oriented language rights is focused primarily on freedom from discrimination in relation to the use of language in private and public sectors, as well as in civil society. In contrast, the debate over promotion-oriented language rights concerns putative responsibilities of the state to create and maintain linguistic domains in minority languages so that language minority groups can enjoy the freedom to participate equally in the life of the polity (p. 145).

9. In May 1991, President Lee Teng-hui canceled the Period of Mobilization for the Suppression of Communist Rebellion, unilaterally ending China's civil war. No longer would the ROC claim to be the rightful government of all of China. Instead, ROC leaders took the line that China was divided into two areas under the jurisdiction of two states. ROC spokesman Jason Hu said in 1993, "We recognized that communist authorities were a political entity. We accepted the fact that the nation was divided, and that, prior to the unification of China, both the ROC and the Chinese communists exercise political authority in the areas under their de facto control. Each is entitled to represent the residents of the territory under its de facto control and to participate in the activities of the international community" (Rigger 1999, p. 154, quoted from Jason Hu, speech dated September 23, 1993, Government Information Office, p. 5).

Chapter 6
A Hybrid Chinese for the Twenty-first Century

Introduction

In this concluding chapter, we summarize major findings from previous chapters and use them to build a concept of "hybrid Chinese"—a de-nationalized and hybridized Mandarin drawing upon features from both local and global interactions as well as a concentric and marginalized identity more compatible than its predecessor, Standard Chinese, in multilingual and multicultural contexts. In addition, we explain the implications for a Greater China[1] (*Dazhonghua* in Chinese). We argue that construction and perceptions of language and identity parallel socio-political transformations, and that language and identity crises arise during power transitions. Under these premises language and identity are never well-defined or well-bounded. In Taiwan's modern history, they have been used as political symbols subject to manipulation and exploitation during socio-historical upheavals. Yet, with democratization and demands for pluralism, alternative ways to conceive of language and identity are being considered in order to maintain a balance of national cohesion while catering to ethnic equality in a multicultural context.

We further argue that what we have learned from Taiwan's experience with socio-political transformation since the island's modernization, starting under Japanese colonization in the late nineteenth century and continuing through regime changes to the democratization that is well under way today, have had profound consequences on the formation and evolution of identity and language. Twice-over monolingualism in the twentieth century created "minorities" whose indigenous language use and cultural practices were perceived, compared with the prevailing national language practice, as deviously abnormal and threatening to national unity. A nationalistic model of language with an intrinsic link to monolithic identity remains problematic in Taiwan not only because of past wrongs done to groups who speak Hakka, Tai-yu, or aboriginal languages but also because of the continuous problems posed by Taiwan's ambiguous nation/state status in the international community. Much has changed since the end of the twentieth century with demands for plurality and space for transnational transaction continuing to gain momentum; yet, ironically, ethnolinguistic struggles among the previously marginalized groups seem also caught in the bind of a nationalistic mode. That is, for the minority language groups, a two way race seems under way from both the macro and the micro levels. On the one hand, they have to compete with other local languages to maintain their "minority" status quo in the centripetal indigenization tide, while on the other, they have to contend with hegemonic languages such as English, Mandarin, or Japanese constituting an outward, centrifugal, and globalization tide. In light of the resulting sets of dilemmas and paradoxes, we propose a hybrid Chinese with poly-center norms in its linguistic stock as well as a mixture of local and global features and a marginal identity not based on pre-determined blood, kinship or ancestral place. Rather, it is based on more pragmatic features such as geopolitics and common roots in order to maintain national unity while still providing a multicultural identity in both social and economic terms. In addressing these issues, we will look into both the global social and cultural trends in language and identity, most notably the concept of a global "Cultural China" proposed by Tu Weiming (1994) and the profound questions it raises for Greater China as observed by Harding (1993) to see if a parallel change has not already taken place on the island. Moreover, we scan a developed international community where similar changes have developed, for example, alternative ideologies of *la francophonie* (Heller 1999) in Canada. These comparisons should bring more resonance to the conclusions of this chapter and their relevance for other Chinese communities.

In addition to the findings of previous chapters, the concepts of hybrid Chinese and marginal identity draw strength from the untapped linguistic aspects of Greater China's various themes (Harding 1993), a discussion of "The Construction of Chinese and Non-Chinese Identities" (Wu 1994), an additional discussion, "On the Margins of the Chinese Discourse" (Lee 1994), and Zhang's argument for a supra-local or transnational linguistic markets in which a "standard" language variety (of a nation-state or a territorially-based community) may not be the "standard" against which values of other varieties are compared and established (cf. Zhang 2005, p. 458). Moreover, we draw our inspiration from the language situation in Canada where similar ethnolinguistic struggles among English and French speakers have been noted (see Chapter 4) and where a post-modern, post-national mode of language and identity has already been documented by scholars (cf. Heller 1999, 2003). More discussion of these ideas and their implications for a linguistic Greater China will follow a summary of chapter findings to this point.

Major Findings from the Chapters

As early as Chapter 1 we observed how political tensions over a center for a standard language and the on-going friction between the CCP and the KMT posed problems for a choice of linguistic features. Apart from the rivalry between Beijing and Taipei, linguistic shibboleths were seen to reveal a quasi Tower of Babel situation belying the concept of Chinese varieties—mutual unintelligibility, after all, is repeatedly reported by speakers of southern varieties such as Cantonese, Hakka, Tai-yu, vis à vis their northern counterpart, Mandarin. The southern varieties' marginalized status has inspired some language groups to try to elevate their social and political status as ethnolinguistic divisions emerged and electoral mobilizations became part of the democratization process.

In Chapter 2, we looked into the choice and usage of more than one language (i.e. the phenomenon of codeswitching) in either daily transactions or in specialized occasions such as political discourse. In addition to presenting a sociolinguistic profile of the island, we extended our analyses of language usage to the more volatile political scene. Most of the literature on codeswitching has treated it from a functional approach, seeing the use of different languages as producing complementary social purposes or as conversational strategies. Few have drawn ideas from sociology and the socio-historical tensions among speakers of different languages, linking such use and choice of language to power relations and contention for resources and representation. In contrast, Heller (1988, 1995) on the language situation in Canada among the anglophones, francophones and the allophones has been most relevant for the discussions and findings in this book. The privilege to use more than one language doesn't come without a sociopolitical price or historical baggage. Historically a heavy handed monolingual policy by both the Japanese and KMT administrations in Taiwan saw Chinese and aboriginal languages in the one case, or Japanese or Chinese varieties other than Mandarin as well as the aboriginal languages in the second case, as threats or impediments to assimilation. The use of any tongue other than the "national language" might subject speakers to suspicion or punishment. Speaking two or more languages was not a choice but a consequence of political liberation. Yet, in a twist of fate and with a dollop of skillful manipulation, the use of a previously marginalized language today can serve as a powerful political symbol to break or make boundaries as well as to evade responsibility (at least temporarily) for addressing the island's problems.

In Chapter 3, we analyzed deliberate choices between Guoyu and Tai-yu made by President Chen Shui-bian during political campaigns. We adopted concepts such as accommodation and Rational Choices to facilitate our analyses. As we found, Chen is unique both politically and linguistically. It was his lot to twice serve as a "minority" president whose slim electoral pluralities left him with no choice but to work with a majority of powerful politicians from the opposition KMT, capable of challenging bills and reforms in the Legislative Yuan. Some factions in the DPP party continued to promote the radical independence movement, which made Chen more enemies both domestically and internationally. His linguistic skills, superb in their use of local idioms and in coining slogans in Tai-yu, won him hearts and minds from grass-root voters while further setting him apart from many other politicians more fluent in English, Guoyu or

Japanese. Seen from this context, Chen's code switching between Guoyu and Tai-yu staged unusually symbolic acts helpful to his seeking allies, pleasing foes and forging temporary alliances.

In Chapter 4, the choice of either Guoyu or Tai-yu was linked to the choice by presidential candidates of endorsing either a China-center policy or Taiwan-based rule. The analyses were made possible by deriving the meaning of a language choice from contingent socio-historical moments and appraising the different political inclinations of the KMT and the DPP. In addition, we tried to depict the meaning of "becoming Taiwanese" as the idea has evolved since its first maturation in the 1920s. Lastly, we concluded that adopting Guoyu and Tai-yu to articulate different political ideals can be seen not just as a promising language strategy for aspiring politicians but as something appealing to the people of the island, many of whom see the ambiguities and indeterminacy of speaking the two as a way out of a simmering ideological cauldron.

In Chapter 5, we tried to see beyond the notion of language as a political symbol, first by stepping back and surveying the language situation in Taiwan since the Dutch and Spanish colonizations in the sixteenth century and subsequent situations through the late nineteenth century, comparing those with the twice over monolingualism imposed by the Japanese and the KMT administrations by turns after 1895. Moreover, we looked into the many changes in language and identity evolving in a post-nationalistic period as the twenty-first century began. We also compared Taiwan's Mandarin-only or Mandarin-plus policies to those of the English-only or English-plus debates in the United States and to institutionalized bilingualism in Canada in order to bring more objectivity to the current dilemma facing Taiwan. In the field of policy changes, we focused on the extent to which a Mandarin-plus policy and concentric identity formation have also been implemented by the Ministry of Education besides noting the setting up of committees to represent the interests of previously marginalized groups and correct the many past wrongs generated in the nationalistic periods. These pluralistic adaptations of language and identity formation certainly have brought Taiwan to a "post-modern" or "post-nationalistic" mode with the notion of a strict nation-state now seen either as passé or an untenable ideal. There are further implications for the interactions in the transnational Chinese community or Greater China. We will spell out them out in the next section.

A Linguistic Greater China

As briefly noted at the beginning of this chapter, increasing interactions among individuals in transnational Chinese communities have prompted many scholars to contemplate the implications for the people of these various communities. For our analysis, we mainly focus on the interactions among China, Hong Kong, and Taiwan. Among the most discussed, cultural, economic and political implications have received the most attention, but a linguistic account of these interactions has been conspicuously missing. Although a clear account of such a void hasn't been found, given the fact that language has been used as a powerful political symbol for the construction of nationalism and essentialized identity in Taiwan's modern history we think it best to combine some of the cultural and political inferences behind Greater China idea to the previous findings of this book, to offer the new idea of a possible linguistic Greater China.

According to Harding (1993), the term Greater China in fact subsumes three distinct, although related, concepts. Economically, Greater China involves the expanding commercial interactions among mainland China, Taiwan and Hong Kong. Culturally, it refers to the restoration of personal, scientific, intellectual and artistic contacts among people of Chinese descent around the world. Politically, it refers to the possibility of the re-establishment of a single Chinese state, reuniting a political entity that disintegrated during more than a century of foreign pressure and civil war. To a degree, the three themes are interrelated: a common cultural identity provides a catalyst for economic ties, and in economic interdependence may lie the foundation for political unification. In theory, therefore, the three aspects of Greater China could merge into a single integrated entity (pp. 683-84).

Seen from a Taiwan voter's perspective, the island's increasing economic dependence and common cultural ties with mainland China have become more important for interactions and transactions with the mainland, but the political aspects might still pose problems. With Taiwan's current national status remaining so ambiguous, immediate reunification under a single Chinese state or a drastic declaration of an independent Taiwan might well be detrimental to both the stability and prosperity of the people on the island. Apprehension and uncertainty over the political cross-Strait situation naturally have bred reservations about what might come next, and no unanimity among the Chinese communities has been forged yet. For example, in mainland China, there is interest in extensive cultural and economic interaction among the People's Republic, Taiwan and Hong Kong, but largely as a way of securing political reunification. On Taiwan, there is also an interest in promoting cultural and economic ties with the mainland, but these are widely regarded as an alternative to political reunification, rather than as a means of achieving it. In Hong Kong, the greatest interest is in the development of economic and cultural ties with South China, largely as a method for cushioning the transfer of political sovereignty to Beijing that occurred in 1997 (cf. Harding 1993, pp. 684-85).

The Good, Bad and Ugly of Longing and Belonging in Times of Uncertainty

Inviting socio-economic conditions and the indeterminacy of a possible political solution resonate very much with what has taken place on Taiwan's current language and identity scene. We suggest that language and the national identity/identities problem are the best places to observe tension and contention for resources and legitimacy in the midst of socio-political change. Academic bickering between essentialism and anti-essentialism in language and linguistics might be "over the top" for most people exposed to an increasingly globalized world, but the die hard arguments that are used to support the China-center ideology and the Taiwan ideology remain insidious. The former believers advocate the continuity and sovereignty of a culture and language, fixed in a preset place and unbroken in history. In contrast, the latter school is preoccupied with contingencies and indeterminacy, and tends to be shrewd and pragmatic. These two seemingly unresolved views still manifest themselves in daily discourse in Taiwan. Even with the end of the colonial regimes, Japanese and Chinese, in the past century and well into the new century, many are very much caught up in essentialized experiences or completely turned off by them. This crops up in virtually every choice and decision that the people of Taiwan make, however mundane or eminent—to -er or not to -er, to speak Mandarin or Tai-yu, to be Chinese or Taiwanese.

In the last century on Taiwan, competing nationalistic visions helped create distinct national and linguistic categories, each one buttressed with arguments that it alone represented a well-defined continuous civilization, high culture and standard language. For much of the rest of the world, strong nationalism and patriotism have always been very much a by-product of the embattled mentality needed to justify reasons for war or military aggression or to buttress a foreign or ethnic minority's rule. These nationalistic visions seem banal when reflected upon rationally and with a clear conscience. In the case of Taiwan, the legacy of civil war between the CCP and the KMT spread over much of the last century and still carries on in the twenty-first, exerting its influence on a host of issues including those related to language and identity. In fact, language varieties and social groups struggling for resources, legitimacy, and representation make nationalist visions prime targets for conflict and contention. These have been recurring themes in Taiwan's modern history: how and why a certain group or linguistic variety has gained in privilege while others have been marginalized or treated prejudicially. The themes tell much about wars won or lost, regimes legitimized or dismissed, and resources withheld or distributed.

We learned that, throughout the course of the twentieth century, whether it was Japaneseness, Chineseness, or Taiwaneseness, all in their most quintessential form manifested a monolithic identity and thereby created ambivalence among the island's people (Brown 1996, Ching 2001, Chang 2003). Worse, clashing expectations and conflicting political ideals arose, challenging the hegemony of the monolithic mentality of Japaneseness and Chineseness during their heyday. This was a fate that awaited, too, the rise of an independent Taiwan consciousness after the 1970s, regardless of the many social and economic advances made during local administrations and the many sacrifices made by their political radicals.

The KMT should have learned these historical lessons well, first with their loss of the civil war to the Communists in the 1940s, then with their reluctant handing over power to the DPP following the 2000 presidential election. The new century offered fertile ground for an all encompassing nationalism: in the remaining backwardness of China compared with the continuing modernity of the West, in the change of political power involving questions of legitimacy, and in the consolidation of ethos crucial to rule. Emotions were raw, and excruciatingly radical ideas for reforms and revolution were rampant. Nationalistic narratives dwelling on past glories and projecting visionary futures were not only politically necessary but offered themselves as psychological panaceas. As Smith (1993) put it succinctly, "Transcending oblivion through posterity; the restoration of collective dignity through an appeal to a golden age; the realization of fraternity through symbols, rites and ceremonies, which bind the living to the dead and fallen of the community: these are the underlying functions of national identity and nationalism in the modern world, and the basic reasons why the latter has proved so durable, protean and resilient through all vicissitudes" (1993, p. 163).

Taiwan's nationalistic narratives in the twentieth century grandly tell of becoming Japanese during the last period of the Japanese occupation (1937-1945), of the importance of being Chinese during the heyday of KMT rule (1949-1987), as well as of the coming to terms with what had always been Taiwanese as the island's young democracy took hold (2000 till now). These nationalistic narratives not only reflected the historical conditions under which the colonial politics of nationalism played out, but also enable people today to weigh the political possibilities of postcolonial identity politics. With political liberation and economic growth, many in Taiwan are opting for a more pragmatic and less nationalistic identity that won't confine them to previous mistakes or leave them caught between impasses with both the transnational and international communities. Yet, some are still charged with grievances over ethno-linguistic injustice, or aggravated by the daily hype and sensationalism of the new election driven culture. More pragmatic oriented metaphors in language and identity might help to distance ourselves from fatalistic nationalistic modes.

In Search of "Post-national" Chinese

With regime transitions, new economic-political forces are playing out both at the national and international levels, but identity politics remains high on the agenda in many transactions. What then are these new forces and contingencies? Can we find a way out of talking about and perceiving identity from the old, fatalistic nationalistic mode? Transnationally, China's ambiguous relationship with Taiwan remains a factor generating serious apprehension. An intimate trading partnership has been and will be vital for Taiwan's economic future, but it will only come if Taiwan modifies its status quo stance in return for more international trade. Many would expect a "Greater China" federal model, imperfectly illustrated in Hong Kong or Singapore, with economic integration but also with political autonomy assured. Different colonial histories aside, Hong Kong's persistent demand for greater democratic freedoms in the years since 1997 hasn't proved very productive. Meanwhile Singapore, an independent city-state fully accepted by the international community, with an ethnic Chinese majority holding position, influence and standing, has never been ruled by the PRC, nor has it been conceived as part of Chinese territory, yet Singapore still controls things such as freedom of speech and the press, at least to a certain extent. Despite optimism and rational choices, China's increasing defense spending—the world's No. 4 after that of the U.S., Britain, and France[2]—and its unfaltering view on how to deal with Taiwan should the island declare independence[3]—remains imminently threatening.

Internationally, the U.S.'s ambiguous relationship with Taiwan is an additional source of concern. The U.S., like most of the rest of the world, officially honors the One China policy formula under which Taiwan is considered by the PRC to be a renegade province, and the problem of reunification is to be solved by both sides of the Strait through peaceful negotiations. But the U.S. has been the biggest arms exporter to Taiwan since it broke diplomatic ties with the island in the 1970s, and it is still urging Taiwan to arm more.[4]

Nationally, many radicals are discontent with the fact that despite efforts for democratization, a genuine Taiwanese state has not been founded. The current state in name and in substance, the ROC (Republic of China), is still a model or shell left over from the KMT regime. The DPP president, having been reelected for a second term, has been contemplating changes to the constitution and to the island's name, initiatives that would be sure to provoke Beijing. However, nobody is sure when or if he will try to carry out such plans.

A zero-sum game mentality is implied by each of these options, and the consequences of making either choice might be too grave. To claim that Taiwan is a pawn in international geopolitics, or to pity it for its wrongful will to embark on a journey of no return, would miss the point. Most of the former colonies of the old colonial powers experienced similar situations culturally, linguistically and politically in the twentieth century. The same blood and soil metaphor used by the Japanese and the KMT to assimilate the Taiwanese to Japanese or Chinese models was used by the Nazis in Germany and the Afrikaners in South Africa. After World War II, most aspiring democratizing countries experienced similar uncertainty when faced with their new found destiny, and none has journeyed free from pain and agony. The breakup of the USSR in the 1980s remains an object lesson in how totalitarianism cannot hold when freedom of choice establishes a sufficient beachhead. Witnessing power transfers to peoples once despised seems trivial compared with what individuals experience at their very base of being, knowing, and speaking. Identity crises always arise during political transitions. Yet, unlike the situation in most new democracies today, in Taiwan the current administration's relationship with China, the U.S. and the majority of the world[5] has created obstacles to the island enjoying the many things others take for granted—participation in international organizations such as the World Health Organization, for example. Ambivalence and indeterminacy still underlie every choice and decision made about politics, identity, and language.

Given the complex geopolitical situation and the potentially huge consequences of charging forward with nationalistic agendas, we think it is important for Taiwan and the Chinese world to find alternative ways to perceive language and identity, ways that encourage practical and economical aspects of identity formation among Chinese. Turning again to the metaphors used in the Chinese case, we argue that most of these are archaic and only play to nationalistic ideologies. They all falsely claim a familial relation among different language groups and insist on a common distinct writing system descriptive of an unbroken history. By deconstructing these myths, it should be possible to come to more practical and rational terms with the reality of the twenty-first century.

Chinese Languages or Dialects?

As noted in Chapter 1, Li (2004) states that political unity, genetic affiliation and shared orthography decide whether two speech varieties are to be labeled dialects of the same language or not. Thus under the Chinese system, "Chinese" is considered a single "language," with Mandarin, Wu, Min, Yue, Xiang, Gan and Hakka being mere dialects of that language, a classification differing markedly from the western approach to the issue, which treats "Chinese" as a language family and Mandarin, Wu, Min, Yue, Xiang, Gan, and Hakka as separate languages, considering that they are not mutually intelligible despite shared orthography and common roots (2004, p. 111).

Many in Taiwan see such a hierarchical model of the Chinese languages as nothing more than a political ploy to subordinate speakers of Tai-yu and Hakka. According to Hsiau (1997), the promoters of the Tai-yu movement reject the official definition of Tai-yu as a "dialect." For them, bilingual education[6] and the establishment of a Tai-yu pronunciation and writing system are crucial to the rebirth of the language. The movement has posed a threat to the status of Mandarin as the national language, the symbol of Chinese identity and a vehicle of political dominance by the Nationalist Party. He further points out that the Tai-yu language movement shares with the official policy a language ideology which is based on the nation-state idea. The dynamics of the Tai-yu language movement reveal a pressing problem facing Taiwan: how to balance national cohesion with multilingualism and multiculturalism (cf. p. 302).

Others criticize the family metaphor by pointing out that by making such an analogy Chinese authorities evoke a primordial sense in language classification, further compounding the effects on a speaker's psyche and perception. Tu (1994) states that the potential for language, especially in its incarnation as the mother tongue, to evoke sympathetic responses or great indignation is great. This matter is compounded by the fact that written Chinese, as a distinct cultural symbol significantly different from an alphabetic system, gives literate Chinese a strong sense of membership in a unique discourse community. These primordial ties—ethnic, territorial, linguistic—are so invested with personal feelings that they almost never present themselves simply as unambiguous conditions of human life (1994, vi). With Tai-yu and Hakka speakers and the aboriginal interest groups becoming more vocal and gaining more influence, distinctive history and writings have been rediscovered and documented. Though their social status might not challenge that of Mandarin in the near future, the very existence and legitimacy of languages different in all forms other than hegemonic ideology is undeniable. The family allusion is complicated by the fact that Beijing, unlike Rome when it was the political center of the western world, has been at war, hot and cold, with its counterparts in Taipei since the 1940s.

Ongoing contention for political domination aside, more logistical items remain for the Tai-yu, Hakka and aboriginal language movements' quests for recognition. With the current improved language policies, tolerance rights have been granted in concert with internationally sanctioned laws and regulations (see Chapter 5), and "mother tongue" education programs have been created and duly implemented and enforced. Problems for the languages' newly elevated status and continuous demands by their speakers for more advantages are not unique to Taiwan, but have occurred in other parts of the world where the entry into a post-colonial era has invigorated many a minority language movement (Fishman 1989). Concerned scholars have voiced their reservations about such contests between the "dominant" language in a post-modern era and modernization or authenticity on the other. Moreover, competing norms and a lack of consensus for the written representation for Tai-yu or Hakka, as well as whether Chinese characters and/or which phonetic scripts should be used (Chiung 2001, Tiu 1998) further complicate the matter. For instance, Huang (2000), trying to depict the conflict between language and identity in Taiwan, observes that local languages are simultaneously facing stiff competition on two fronts. They have had to contend not only with Mandarin, the official language, for breathing space, but also with international languages, especially English and, to a lesser extent, Japanese, for survival, as entrepreneurial Taiwan has become further enmeshed in international trade and politics. To the extent that English is the lingua franca of modern business and scientific and diplomatic intercourse, the move toward "mother tongue education" in the elementary school curriculum is seen by some as a step backward (p. 146). In addition, Huang, citing Fishman on the minority language movements (1989, p. 126) explains the dilemma in terms of "the tension between the major requirements of modernization and those of authentification.... While the first is constantly straining toward newer, more rational, more efficient solutions to the problems of today and tomorrow, the second is constantly straining toward pure, more genuine expression of the heritage of yesterday and of long ago" (cf. 2000, p. 146).

From Nationalism to Multiculturalism

While the prevailing political indeterminacy might freeze many of us from offering any clear cut solutions, economic and cultural interactions seem relatively pragmatic and straightforward, offering breathing room for Greater China transitionally and internationally. For instance, the most recent analyses of economic trends foresee the development of several different economic regions, each linking segments of the transnational Chinese economy to economic systems where ethnic Chinese do not play a dominant role. Similarly, discussion of cultural matters is increasingly acknowledging that Chinese living outside mainland China are probably developing and will maintain a multi-layered cultural identity, viewing themselves both as Chinese and Taiwanese, or Chinese and American, or Chinese and whatever, rather than as Chinese alone (Harding 1993, p. 685).

The last two points run parallel to recent developments in Taiwan on pluralism in language and identity formation. Linguistically, people have tried to cope by switching to either Guoyu or Tai-yu as occasions demand, thus escaping the hot pot of reunification or independence ideological choices. Switching between different languages in a democratized context can be used to enact social values and express a plurality of cultural categories. Strategically, given the history of Taiwan with its ambiguous status internationally and its contentious ethnic relations domestically, language choices can be and are abused to polarize perspectives and politicize ethnic relations for political gain. Our analyses of the language choices by some of the most prominent politicians reveal just how much such verbal ingenuity can be marshaled to strike at the political nerves of constituents and thus mobilize/polarize votes. Much of this psychological power is derived from historical memories and the political positions people take, positions further embedded in the ambiguities and indeterminacy associated with alternations between Guoyu and Tai-yu, the former being associated with cultural determinism and the latter with political pragmatism. The situation in Taiwan is therefore similar to, yet much more volatile than, what has been proposed in Canada's Quebec Province and in Shenzhen, China. With the very notion of Taiwan independence construed as an invitation for military intervention from Beijing, and unification as termination of democracy and sovereignty, alternating between Guoyu and Tai-yu, and perhaps English and Japanese to a lesser extent, is seen as a practical and political necessity to make friends and appease foes.

In addition, Guoyu has also taken on many local features and has incorporated foreign influences, mostly from English and Japanese, to meet the demands of sophisticated speakers from Taipei and the other side of the Strait. This hybridized Taiwan Mandarin is no longer based on a single political center; rather it draws its currency and resonance from not only local languages such as Tai-yu, Hakka and aboriginal languages but also phonological and lexical features from Shanghai, Shenzhen, and Hong Kong. Although systematic research on a linguistic model for Greater China has not yet been established, scholarly works such as those by Zhang (2005) and Li (2004) have already pointed out possible directions for its development. Scholars of languages in contact have long documented the indigenization of Mandarin in various communities (Cheng 1999; Kubler 1981, 1985). A hybrid Chinese that cuts across geographical boundaries and beyond ethno-linguistic determination might be a way out for the cause of increasing contacts between Beijing and Taipei as well as for a people facing multiple language choices in their daily transactions. In fact, Zhang (2005) advocates a cosmopolitan Mandarin like the one that has been practiced by Beijing professionals, which is to say a hybrid Chinese mixed with features from Hong Kong and Taiwan Mandarin as well as a sprinkling of English expressions. On a similar note, Li (2004) points out that we may be witnessing the rise of a modern Chinese educated accent that cuts across geographical boundaries among news media anchorpersons on both sides of the Taiwan Strait. The end result may be the development of middle-class urban varieties of Chinese that are generally much more similar to one another all across China than they are to local working-class or rural varieties (cf. 2004, p. 128).

With such linguistic adaptations to a plural and cosmopolitan context there might come additional political gains. A de-colonized, poly-centered hybrid Chinese might discount the prejudice in Taiwan against Mandarin as a "Beijing dialect," thus unfit for its current default status as an official language. Languages might be recognized for what they are, divisive symbols with inherent flaws of arrogance and destructiveness to others. On the other hand, an intrinsic link between an official language, an essentialized identity and a zero-sum mentality might confound such possibilities. The ultimate result might bring Taiwan to the verge of the biblical scene of the Tower of Babel, where the curse of confusion might prove that none of the above (Tai-yu for the independence minded, Hakka and the aboriginal languages for the splittists, and Mandarin or Japanese for the déjà vu colonials) can survive the tasks of communicating truly and behaving civilly in the twenty-first century.

Venturing beyond the Tower of Babel teaching, we now turn to a modern scene in a more developed country, Canada, in order to pinpoint more objective alternatives to intrinsic links between language and identity. In Canada, a postnational relationship among speakers of English, French and other languages has been well-documented, and this transformation can shed light on "minority" language movements as opposed to languages with official status such as Mandarin. Heller (1999, 2003b) offers an alternative ideology of *la francophonie* and explains why it relates to Western linguistic minorities in general. By adopting Gramscian's[7] notion of hegemony as well as Giddens (1990)'s[8] concept of high modernity, Heller (1999) points out that ideologies of language and national identity are changing as part of globalization, characterized by the breaking down of modern ideologies of language and the nation state. Her thesis is further supported with ethnographic fieldwork that examines the ways in which the institutionalized structures related to *la francophonie* have been called into question by ongoing political economic change. With respect to Western linguistic minorities (and perhaps linguistic minorities elsewhere, too), we learn that modernist nationalist ideologies which have served local bourgeoisies so well are now being called into question by high modernity (1999, p. 356). The story of linguistic minorities can be told as a story of the ways in which hyper-modernity is transforming relations of power and the bases of identity in the Western world (2003b, p. 3). Moreover, as the author states:

> ". . . the old politics of identity which situated [francophone Canada] in the world and gave it a basis from which to fight for what it wanted, is being challenged in three ways. First, it is being challenged from within, as unity gives way to diversity. Second, it is being challenged from without, as the old structures in which the politics of identity made sense, in particular state structures, give way to new forms of social organization and values based on corporate capitalism. Third, it is being challenged by its own success, as the authenticity of its past gives way to entry into the modern world. What happens to these voyagers, that is, the path they choose to (and are able to) navigate [toward] opportunities and around obstacles, the goals they set for themselves and their ability to achieve them, is part of the story of what is happening to minorities around the world, as the world changes shape (*ibid*: pp. 4-5)."

Heller's work is most helpful not only because the situations and linguistic choices for Canadians between French and English bear similarities to those between Mandarin and Tai-yu in daily transactions in Taiwan (see Chapter 4), but also because she shows that directions and challenges of identity politics belie ethnolinguistic struggles in a new era. Moreover the changing meanings, constructions and strategies of being or doing *"la francophonie"* bring insights for Taiwanese. The challenges from within and without to a single notion of Taiwanese as opposed to Chinese, and the many forces involved—nationalism, democracy, multiculturalism locally and globally—share similar effects with the challenges of exercising *"la francophonie."*

To return to the Taiwan scene, Tai-yu and its cultural practices to most radicals have been associated with independence since the Japanese colonization. Such discourse, so counter to the Japanese and Chinese dominant political discourses, did not start to escape fully into the open until the lifting of martial law in 1987 when speaking different tongues in public became part of the overall political scene, testing the then ruling KMT's tolerance of freedom of press and speech, challenging its legitimacy, and challenging as well the official status of Mandarin, ever the "Beijing dialect" to some. Political symbols were redefined and reinterpreted to articulate these voices of pluralism.

Language and ethnic boundaries have now been recalibrated, negotiated and redrawn. Policies on language and ethnicity have been revised to compensate for the past wrongs of neglecting and subordinating Chinese dialects, aboriginal languages and the languages of underrepresented groups such as the Hakka. When power loses its base at the top, consequences follow for language issues. Monolingualism has been replaced with multilingualism, at least in offering tolerance rights and a forum for polyphony. Standardization, or better yet the new question of which standard variety, if any, one should adhere to, draws attention and generates heated debate from not only politicians and scholars but from many interest groups, too. A scene is created that resonates deeply back to the days of China's May Fourth movement when *baihua* (plain speech) was replacing *wenyan* (the classic language) for the sake of spreading crucial concepts such as science and democracy (Chen 1999). Despite seeming disparities in terms of language choices on the mainland then and in Taiwan now—in 1919 progressives were trying to change the written standard of Chinese to base it more on *baihua*, while today in Taiwan they are trying to accommodate speakers of formerly marginalized vernaculars with their increasing demands for representation in a democratized twenty-first century—nevertheless, the two situations are parallel in showing what politics has done, can do and will do to alter language in modern Chinese history. Today, the enemy is not the Japanese or western aggressors from without but adversaries within. In light of the new political alliances, Mandarin and Tai-yu, and Hakka to a lesser extent, are no longer seen as members within the same language family. Each rides on a democratic tide, contending for power and resources. The dynamics among these competitions and their quest for representation and resources cannot be ignored. The language classification metaphor of the family grossly overlooks this fact. In its place a more economics-oriented metaphor is needed to reflect the long concealed reality of Chinese language varieties and the need for a multilingual-based language policy that is not hegemonic or exclusive, one that will ensure that people will not be discriminated against or marginalized based on the language used. Moreover, this should not contradict an emphasis on proficiency in a polycentric standard language valuable not for "nationalistic" purposes but for economic and practical reasons apparent to speakers from different parts of China.

Ambiguities in Identity Politics

Whether it's to be a marginal multi-centered cultural China or a hybrid Chinese speaking Greater China, both possibilities run parallel to the modern identity politics we are seeing. Much of the ongoing political discourse in Taiwan is now focused on redefining the monolithic, China-centered nationalism and Han-dominant cultural monopoly that dominated most of the twentieth century on both sides of the Taiwan Strait. A "post-national" pragmatism as defined in Corcuff (2002) has entered the cultural-political discourse. Forms of association with China have been conceived and issues of identification have been reengineered according to a theory of concentric spheres encompassing the local (i.e. Taiwan), the cultural (the Chinese world), and the global (the world itself)—three concentric horizons of identification, suitable to be cultivated by Taiwanese youth (2002, p. 247).

This new formula for a renewed identity quest derives from a politics of difference enriched with economic-political pragmatism vis-à-vis China. People in Taiwan are now positioned to take stock of various contributions to their history—those of the Dutch and Spanish colonists, the Japanese imperialists, the KMT, the DPP, and the aboriginals long marginalized. In light of such a multi-centered and multi-layered identification embedded in the new Taiwan identity, we think it is very advantageous to adopt the "marginality" concept from anthropology as a theoretical apparatus to better understand the complexity of Taiwan identity politics.

According to Lee (1994), when discussing Chinese identity, more thought should be given to the concept of the marginality of self-identity. Marginality can be defined as one's own ambiguous status of belonging simultaneously to more than one collective entity. For any of these entities, the identity is incomplete (1994, p. 239).

Marginality is closely related to the dichotomy of a center and its peripheries. A center and its peripheries need not be viewed as contradiction and confrontation; they are merely relative positions in a continuum. The center, be it geographic, geopolitical, social-economic, or even cultural-ideological, possesses a gravitational force which pulls from the peripheries whatever elements are scattered therein. The continuous centripetal attraction leads to an increase in the size and the mass of the center, which eventually incorporates the peripheries completely to form a new, bigger center with an even more powerful gravitational force (ibid, p. 240).

In light of Taiwan's ambiguous socio-political context, the marginality concept not only helps to disentangle layers of identifications—cultural, ethnic, and political—but also helps one understand that the relationship between a center and its peripheries (which can have multiple definitions given Taiwan's tumultuous modern history) is always in transition and transformation. The liberties and ambiguities to be found in such illumination are thus seen as far more appropriate than continuing to perceive ethnic identity as determined by ancestral origin, cultural identity as invariant sets of practices, and political identity as a preemptive act.

The "New Taiwanese" identity should further facilitate interactions with and among other Chinese communities and might contribute to their development in identity formation. In addition, the concept runs parallel to other identity politics in the most developed parts of the world. To illustrate our first point, we return to the idea of Tu Wei-ming (1994) of a "Cultural China" with which a non-ethnic based identity can be conceived. *Huaren* is not geopolitically centered, for it only indicates a common ancestry and a shared cultural background (p. 25). Nevertheless, the non-exclusive membership and the elusive idea of a political center have caused scholars such Harding (1993) to ponder the implications for a Greater China, for several profound and interrelated questions are raised. We summarize Harding's observations as follows. First, he points out that Tu defines membership in a global Chinese culture culturally, rather than ethnically: it consists of all those, from whatever ethnic background, who participate in the "international discourse of cultural China" and who thereby join in the creation of a modern Chinese identity. Secondly, the "periphery as the center" subtitle of Tu's article suggests that the "periphery will come to set the . . . cultural agenda for the center." Or as he (Tu) puts it elsewhere, "A significantly weakened center may turn out to be a blessing in disguise for the emergence of a truly functioning Chinese civilization-state." Thirdly, what will the content be of the modern Chinese identity to be produced by the "international discourse of Cultural China?" (cf. Harding 1993, p. 674). In essence, Harding offers that in contrast to neo-authoritarian visions, the prevailing view among Chinese intellectuals in Hong Kong, Taipei and overseas is for a much more democratic version of modern Chinese culture, in step with the organizational and ideological pluralism associated with liberal democracies in the West (cf. p. 675).

To illustrate Harding's second point about the periphery coming to set the agenda for the center, we turn once again to the Canada experience and a French perspective to lend more international resonance to the new trend of hybrid identity formation. Harding's exegesis and the Canada story not only elucidate the insidious ethnocentric byways of nationalistic identity formation but also offer psychological explanations as to why the nationalistic vision has been so hard to get rid of. We turn to Maclure (2003) who represents a new generation of writers concerned with Canadian identity in general and Quebec's uniqueness specifically and who are increasingly frustrated with the dichotomy between, on the one hand, a melancholy nationalistic view rooted in historical French defeat and the minority status of French relative to English, curable only by independence or defiance; and on the other hand a cosmopolitan individualism based on reason and pragmatism that sees Quebec nationalism as parochial, ethnocentric and backward in a society aiming for liberalism. Maclure has tried to argue against the impasse of the two polarizing views, recommending instead the hybridity and ambiguity characteristic of modern identity politics. On a similar note, Lisee (2001) stresses the importance of maintaining Quebec's uniqueness and linguistic equilibrium, and proposes reforms to enhance the security of the linguistic communities by drawing them closer through a shared identity that might stem Quebec's looming demographic decline. Lisee's account speaks to the anxieties and insecurities shared by those undergoing a crisis of identity decline, i.e. francophones, anglophones and allophones. Francophone insecurity arises from the minority status of the *Québécois* in Canada and, even more dramatically, from their minority status in North America as a whole. This insecurity is exacerbated by both a generalized misgiving over the long-run impact of economic and cultural globalization, and by the more concrete fear of soon becoming a minority on the Island of Montreal (ibid, p. 168). The anglophone community meanwhile suffers from its experience of a significant exodus from Quebec Province since 1960. Many of its members continue to depart, especially the young. This community fears for its long-term vitality. It fears that each and every new provincial linguistic initiative will curtail its language rights still further. The allophone communities—those with neither French nor English as the mother tongue—find themselves minorities twice over, torn as they are between their own complex identities and the contradictory expectations of the Québećois and Canadian host societies. They must maneuver in a peculiar, not to say confusing, political and linguistic context (ibid). Lisee's account of the current French Canadian identity and language situation is not only refreshing but also inspiring in that we can see how the drive behind various movements or regulations arises not so much from grand forces—economic and political—as from the individual psyche and its anxieties over shifting identity and language boundaries. It's a fine point that speaks tellingly of those undergoing a language and identity crisis. It's also a recurring theme in Taiwan's modern history and a cautionary tale for an imagined Greater China.

Notes

1. This term, used generally and in a sense most relevant to the discussion in this book, is a tag appropriate for referring to the rapidly increasing interaction among Chinese societies around the world as technical, political and administrative barriers to their interchanges fall (cf. Harding 1993, p. 660). It is also important to note that some don't like the concept of "Greater China" on grounds of desirability or feasibility for regional and global eco-political balances or consequences. Whether "Greater China" will ever be realized or is just a phantom is immaterial to the discussions of this book. We are only interested in the increasing interactions among Chinese across the Strait and their consequences, most importantly on language and identity.
2. According to the Stockholm International Peace Research Institute, in 2006 China (4.3 percent) topped Japan (3.8 percent) to become the world's fourth largest defense spender after America (45.7 percent), Britain (5.1 percent) and France (4.6 percent). (Quoted from *The Economist*, 'American Power: The hobbled hegemony," June 28, 2007 (online edition).
3. John Copper (1996) and many others have reported how the Chinese leaders in Beijing have threatened to invade Taiwan under certain circumstances. Although these threats have varied over time, Beijing basically says it will employ military force against Taiwan if it: 1) allows foreign control, 2) builds nuclear weapons, 3) experiences internal turmoil, 4) declares independence, or 5) refuses to negotiate reunification over a long period of time (p. 179).
4. This came with the normalization of diplomatic ties between Beijing and Washington on January 1, 1979. In April 1979, the Taiwan Relations Law (TRA), the first ever U.S. law establishing guidelines for Washington's relations with another country, was signed by President Carter. For details of the Law, see U.S. statement website http://usinfo.state.gov/eap/Archive_Index/Taiwan_Relations_Act.html. According to Copper (1999), in most respects, the TRA treated Taiwan as a sovereign nation-state; the act certainly did not refer to it as a province of the People's Republic of China—as Beijing contended was Taiwan's status and was stated in the Normalization of 1979. The TRA also normalized economic relations between Taiwan and the U.S. The act thus prevented a crash of investor confidence in Taiwan and served as a signal to U.S. businesses that relations with Taiwan were to remain normal. Trade and U.S. investment in Taiwan in fact increased considerably in ensuing years (ibid, p. 162).
5. Currently, Taiwan has diplomatic ties with twenty-four countries in the world.

6. For details on the problems for bilingual education posed by Tai-yu and Hakka, please refer to Scott and Tiu (2007), pp. 60-62.

7. See Gramsci, Antonio. 1971. *Selections from the Prison Notebooks*. Lawrence and Wishhart.

8. See Giddens, Anthony. 1990. *The Consequences of Modernity*. Cambridge: Polity.

Bibliography

Auer, Peter. *Bilingual Conversation*. John Benjamins, Amsterdam, 1984.
Auer, Peter, ed. *Code-Switching in Conversation: Language, Interaction and Identity*. Routledge, London, 1998.
Bakhtin, M. M. *The Dialogic Imagination*. Austin: University of Texas Press, 1981.
———. *Speech Genres and Other late Essays*. Austin: University of Texas Press, 1986.
Barnes, Dailey. *Language planning in Mainland China: A sociolinguistic study of Putonghua and Pinyin*. Ph.D. dissertation. Georgetown University, 1974.
———. "To er or not to er." *Journal of Chinese Linguistics* 5 (1997): 211-36.
Bateson, Gregory. *Steps to an ecology of mind*. San Francisco: Chandler, 1972.
Berg, M. E. "Language Planning and Language Use in Taiwan: Social Identity, Language Accommodation, and Language Choice Behavior." *International Journal of Sociology of Language*, 59 (1986): 97-115.
Blom, Jan-Petter and John Gumperz. "Social Meaning in Linguistic Structure: Codeswitching in Norway," in *Directions in Sociolinguistics: Ethnography of Communication*, edited by Gumperz, John and Hymes, Dell, New York: Holt, Rinehart and Winston, Inc, 1972.
Bokhorst-Heng and Wendy Diana. *Language and Imagining the Nation in Singapore*. Ph.D. Dissertation. Department of Sociology and Equity Studies. University of Toronto, 1998.
Bourdieu, Pierre. *Outline of a Theory of Practice*. Trans. Richard Nice. Cambridge: Cambridge University Press, 1977.
Bourdieu, Pierre and Loic J. D. Wacquant. *An Invitation to Reflexive Sociology*. Chicago: University of Chicago Press, 1992.
Brown, Melissa, ed. *Negotiating Ethnicities in China and Taiwan*. Institute of East Asian Studies, University of California, Berkeley, 1996.
———. *Is Taiwan Chinese? The Impact of Culture, Power and Migration on Changing Identities*. Berkeley: University of California Press, 2004.
Brown, P., and S. Levinson. *Politeness: Some Universals in Language Use*. Cambridge: Cambridge University Press, 1987.
Buruma, I. "Taiwan's New Nationalists," *Foreign Affairs* 75, no. 4 (1997): 77-91.
Campbell, William. *Formosa under the Dutch: Described from Contemporary Records,*

with Explanatory Notes and a Bibliography of the Island. Taipei: SMC Publishing, 1992.

Chang, Michael Mau-kuei. "The Formation and Predicament of Multiculturalism in Taiwan," [Duoyuan wenhua yu duoyuan zhuyi zai Taiwan de xingcheng yu nanti]. Pp. 223-273 in *The Future of Taiwan [Taiwan de weilai]*, edited by Xue Tien-zhu. Taipei: Huatai Publishing, 2000.

———. "On the Origins and Transformation of Taiwanese National Identity." Pp. 23-58 in *Religion and the Formation of Taiwanese Identities*, edited by Paul R. Katz and Murray A. Rubinstein. New York: Palgrave Macmillan, 2003.

Chang, M. Y. *Language Use and Language Attitudes Among Taiwanese Elementary School Students in Native Language Instruction Programs: A Study on Language Maintenance.* Ph.D. Dissertation. Bloomington, IN: Indiana University, 1996.

Chang, Shu-chen. *Code Mixing of English and Taiwanese in Mandarin Discourse.* MA. Thesis. National Taiwan Normal University, 2000.

Chao, Yuen Ren. *Grammar of Spoken Chinese.* Berkeley: University of California Press, 1968.

———. *Aspects of Chinese Sociolinguistics.* Stanford: Stanford University Press, 1976.

Chen, M. R. *A Study of the Language Educational Policies in Taiwan after Its Retrocession.* Unpublished MA Thesis. English Department, National Taiwan Normal University, 1996.

Chen, Ping. *Modern Chinese: History and Sociolinguistics.* Cambridge: Cambridge University Press, 1999.

———. "Policy on the Selection and Implementation of a Standard Language as a Source of Conflict in Taiwan," Pp. 95-110 in *Language Planning and Language Policy: East Asian Perspectives*, edited by Nanette Gottlieband and Ping Chen. Richmond, UK: Curzon Press, 2001.

Chen, S. C. "Reinvigorating Ethnic Cultural Identity through Mother-tongue Teaching Materials in Taiwan." *Language, Cultural and Curriculum*, 9(3) (1996a): 254-9.

———. "Code-switching as a Verbal Strategy among Chinese in a Campus Setting." *World Englishes*, 15(3) (1996b): 267-280.

Cheng, Allen. "Chen: Pop Icon Piranha." *Asiaweek* 26, No. 12 (March 2000)

Cheng, Robert. "A Comparison of Taiwanese, Taiwan Mandarin, and Peking Mandarin." *Language* 61 (2) (1985):352-77.

———. "Hu tsa te tsu-ti yu chi-hui tu tai-yu hsieh Tai-yu (Let our children have opportunities to read and write Tai-yu)." *Tai-wan wen-i (Taiwan Literature)* 136, (1993): 173-80.

Cheng, Y. S. *A Preliminary Syntactic Study on Mandarin/Taiwanese Code-switching.* Unpublished Master's thesis. National Taiwan Normal University, 1989.

Chilton, P and Ilyin. "Metaphor in Political Discourse." *Discourse and Society*, 4(1) (1993): 7-31.

Ching, Leo T. S. *Becoming "Japanese": Colonial Taiwan and the Politics of Identity Formation.* Berkeley: University of California Press, 2001.

Chiung, W. T. "Language Attitudes Towards Written Taiwanese." *Journal of Multilingual*

and Multicultural Development, 22(2)(2001): 502-521.
Chu, Jou-Jou. "Nationalism and Self-Determination: The Identity Politics." Pp. 303-19 in *Journal of Asian and African Studies* 35 Issue 3, 2000.
Chun, Allen. "Democracy as Hegemony, Globalization as Indigenization, or the 'Culture' in Taiwanese National Politics." Pp. 7-27 in *Journal of Asian and African Studies*, XXXV, 1, 2000.
Coblin, W. "A Brief History of Mandarin." Pp. 537-552 in *Journal of the American Oriental Society*. 120.4, 2000.
Copper, John. *Taiwan: Nation-State or Province?* Boulder, Co: Westview Press, 1996.
Corcuff, Stephane, ed. *Memories of the Future: National Identity Issues and the Search for a New Taiwan*. New York: M. E. Shape, 2002.
———. "The Symbolic Dimension of Democratization and the Transition of National Identity under Lee Teng-hui." Pp. 73-102 in *Memories of the Future*, edited by Stephane Corcuff. New York: M. E. Sharpe, 2002.
———. "Conclusion: History, the Memories of the Future." Pp. 243-252 in *Memories of the Future: National Identity Issues and the Search of a New Taiwan*, edited by Stephane Corcuff. New York: M.E. Sharpe Inc, 2002.
Culler, Jonathan. *Saussure*. Hassocks: Harvester Press, 1976.
DeFrancis, John. *The Chinese Language: Fact and Fantasy*. Honolulu: University of Hawaii Press, 1984.
Erbaugh, Mary S. "Southern Chinese Dialects as a Medium for Reconciliation within Greater China." *Language in Society* 24, (1995): 79-94.
Errington, Joseph. "Colonial Linguistics." *Annual Review of Anthropology*, 30(2001): 19-39.
Fairclough, Norman. *Language and Power*. New York: Longman, 1989.
———. *Discourse and Social Change*. Cambridge: Polity Press, 1992.
Figueroa, E. "Evaluating Language Policy in Taiwan: Some Questions." Pp. 285-299 in *The Structure of Taiwanese: A Modern Synthesis*, edited by Robert Chang and Shuanfan Huang. Taipei: Crane Publishing, Ltd., 1988.
Fishman, Joshua. "Who Speaks What Language to Whom and When?" *Linguistics* 2, (1965): 67–88.
———. "Domains and the Relationship between Micro- and Macro-sociolinguistics." Pp. 435–453 in *Directions in Sociolinguistics*, edited by Gumperz, J. J., Hymes, D. Holt, Rinehart and Winston, New York, 1972.
Fishman, J. A. *Language and Nationalism: Two Integrative Essays*. Rowley, Massachusetts: Newbury House Publishers, 1972.
Fishman, J. A., C. A. Ferguson and J. Das Gupta eds. *Language Problems of Developing Nations*. New York: John Wiley and Sons, 1968.
Friedman, Kerim. "Learning 'Local' Language: Passive Revolution, Language Market, and Aborigine Education in Taiwan." Ph.D. Dissertation. The Temple University, 2005.

Bibliography

Gal, Susan. "The Political Economy of Code Choice." In *Codeswitching: Anthropological and sociolinguistic perspectives,* edited by M. Heller, 245-64. New York: Mouton de Gruyter, 1988.

Giles, H. and P. F. Powesland. *Speech Style and Social Evaluation.* New York: Academic Press, 1975.

Giles, H. and P. M. Smith. "Accommodation Theory: Optimal Levels of Convergence" in *Language and Psychology,* edited by H. Giles and R. Clair. Oxford: Blackwell, 1979.

Greefeld, Karl Taro. "Is Chen the One?" *Time* 157, no. 20 (May 21, 2001)

Gumperz, John. "Conversational Codeswitching." Pp. 59-99 in *Discourse Strategies* by J. Gumperz. Cambridge: Cambridge University Press, 1982.

———. *Discourse Strategies.* New York: Cambridge University Press, 1982.

Gumperz and Hernandez-Chavez. "Cognitive Aspects of Bilingual Communication." *Language and Social Chang,* edited by W. H. Whiteley. Oxford University Press, 115-25, 1975.

Hall, Stuart, and Paul de Gay. *Questions of Cultural Identity.* London: Sage, 1996.

Hanks, William. "Pierre Bourdieu and the Practices of Language," *Annual Review of Anthropology* 34(2005): 67-83.

Harding, Harry 1993. "The Concept of 'Greater China': Themes, Variations and Reservations." Pp. 660-686 in *The China Quarterly,* No. 136, Special Issue: Greater China. (Dec., 1993)

Harrell, Stevan. "Introduction." Pp. 1-18 in *Negotiating Ethnicities in China and Taiwan.* Edited by Melissa Brown. Institute of East Asian Studies, University of California, Berkeley, 1996.

Heath, Shirley Brice. *Ways with Words.* Cambridge: Cambridge University Press, 1983.

Heller, Monica ed. *Codeswitching: Anthropological and Sociolinguistic Perspectives.* New York: Mouton de Gruyter, 1988.

———. "The Politics of Codeswitching and Language Choice." *Journal of Multilingual and Multicultural Development,* Vol. 13, Nos 1&2, (1992): 123-142.

———. "Language choice, social institutions, and symbolic Domination." *Language in Society 24,* (1995): 373-405.

———. "Alternative Ideologies of la francophonie." *Journal of Sociolinguistics,* Vol. 3, Issue 3, (1999): 336-359.

———. *Crosswords: Language, Education and Ethnicity in French Ontario.* Mouton De Gruyter, 2003.

Heylen, Ann. "Dutch Language Policy and Early Formosan Literacy (1624-1662)," Pp. 199-251 in *Missionary Approaches and Linguistics in Mainland China and Taiwan,* edited by Wei-ying Ku. Leuven: Leuven University Press, 2001.

———. "The Legacy of Literacy Practices in Colonial Taiwan. Japanese-Taiwanese-Chinese: Language Interaction and Identity Formation." *Journal of Multilingual and Multicultural Development.* Vol. 26, No. 6. (2005): 496-511.

Bibliography

Hill, Jane. "The Refiguration of the Anthropology of Language." *Cultural Anthropology* 2(1987): 89-103.

Hill, Kenneth C. and Jane H. Hill. *Speaking Mexicano: Dynamics of Syncretic Language in Central Mexico*. Tucson: University of Arizona Press, 1986.

Ho, Szu-yin and I-chou Liu. "The Taiwanese/Chinese Identity of the Taiwan People in the 1990s," *American Asian Review*, Vol. XX, No. 2. Summer, (2002): 29-75.

Hong, Weiren. "Tan Helaoyu de Zheng zi yu yuyuan," [On correct characters and the etymology of Taiwanese]. Pp. 343-362 in *Xiandai Taiwanhua yanjiu lunwen ji* [The Structure of Taiwanese: a modern synthesis], edited by Robert Cheng and Shuanfan Huang. Taipei: Crane Publishing, 1988.

Hornberger, Nancy. "Language Policy, Language Education, Language Rights: Indigenous, Immigrant, and International Perspectives," *Language in Society*, 27, (1998): 439-458.

Hsiao, Hsin-Huang Michael. "Emerging Social Movements and the Rise of a Demanding Civil Society in Taiwan," *The Australian Journal of Chinese Affairs*, no. 24 (July 1990): 163-179.

Hsiau, A-chin. "Language Ideology in Taiwan: The KMT's Language Policy, the Tai-yu Language Movement, and Ethnic Politics," *Journal of Multilingual and Multicultural Development* 18, no. 4 (1997): 302-315.

Huang, Shuan-Fan. *Language, Society and Ethnic Identity: A Sociolinguistic Research on Taiwanese Languages*. Taipei: Crane Publishing, Ltd., 1993.

———. "Language, Identity and Conflict: A Taiwan Study," *International Journal of Sociology of Language* 143 (2000): 139-149.

Hughes, Christopher and Robert Stone. "Nation-Building and Curriculum Reform in Hong Kong and Taiwan." Pp. 977-991 in *The China Quarterly*, 1999.

Jian, S. L. *Code-switched Word Recognition by Taiwanese-Mandarin Bilinguals*. Unpublished MA thesis. Hsinchu Teachers College, 2000.

Kloter, Henning. "Facts and Fantasy about Favorlang: Early European Encounters with Taiwan's Languages." Paper presented at the Second Conference of the European Association of Taiwan Studies Ruhr-University Bochum, April 1-2, 2005.

Koenig, Matthias. "Social Conditions for the Implementation of Linguistic Human Rights Through Multicultural Policies: The Case of the Kyrgyz Republic." *Current Issues in Language and Society* 6, no. 1(1999): 57-84.

Kubler, Cornelieus. *The Development of Mandarin in Taiwan: A Case Study of Language Contact*. Ph.D. Dissertation. Cornell University, 1981.

———. "The Influence of Southern Min on the Mandarin of Taiwan." *Anthropological Linguistics* 27, no. 2 (1985): 156-77.

———. "Codeswitching between Taiwanese and Mandarin in Taiwan." Pp. 263-283 in *The Structure of Taiwanese: A Modern Synthesis*, edited by Huang and Chang. Taipei: Crane Publishing, Ltd., 1988.

Labov, William. *The Social Stratification of English in New York City*. Washington, D.C.: Center for Applied Linguistics, 1966.

———. *The Study of Nonstandard English*. The National Council of Teachers of English by special arrangement with the Center for Applied Linguistics, 1970.

———. *Language in the Inner City*. Philadelphia: University of Pennsylvania Press, 1972.

Lai Tse-han, Ramon H. Myers, and Wei Wou. *A Tragic Beginning: The Taiwan Uprising of February 28, 1947*. Stanford: Stanford University Press, 1991.

Lakoff, Robin. "Women's Language." *Women's Language and Style*, edited by D. Butturff and E. L. Epstein. Akron, Ohio: University of Akron Press, 1979.

Le Page, R.B. and Andree Tabouret-Keller. *Acts of Identity: Creole-based Approaches to Language and Ethnicity*. Cambridge: Cambridge University Press, 1985.

Lee, Leo Ou-fan. "On the Margins of the Chinese Discourse: Some Personal Thoughts on the Cultural Meaning of the Periphery." Pp. 221-241 in *The Living Tree: The Changing Meaning of Being Chinese Today*, edited by Tu Wei-ming. Stanford: Stanford University Press, 1994.

Li, Wei. "The 'Why' and 'How' Questions in the Analysis of Conversational Codeswitching." Pp. 156-179 in *Codeswitching in Conversation: Language, Interaction and Identity*, edited by Peter Auer. New York: Routledge, 1998.

———. "'What do you want me to say?' On the Conversation Analysis Approach to Bilingual Interaction." *Language in Society* 31, (2002): 159–180.

Li, Chris Wen-Chao. "Conflicting Notions of Language Purity: The Interplay of Archaizing, Ethnographic, Reformist, Elitist and Xenophobic Purism in the Perception of Standard Chinese." *Language and Communication* 24 (2004): 97-133.

Li, W., and Lesley Milroy. "Conversational Code-switching in a Chinese Community in Britain: A Sequential Analysis." *Journal of Pragmatics* 23, (1995): 281–299.

Lin, Mei-chun (2002). "Hokkien Should Be Given Official Status, Says TSU (Taiwan Solidarity Union)." *Taipei Times Online Edition*. www.taipeitimes.com/news/2002/03/10/print/0000127068. (accessed March 10, 2002).

Link, Perry, Richard Madsen, and Paul H. Pickowicz. *Unofficial China: Popular Thought and Culture in the People's Republic*. Boulder, CO: Westview Press, 1989.

Lisee, Jean-Francois. "Invest in Quebec's Uniqueness." *Inroads* 10 (2001): 167-186

Maclure, Jocelyn. *Quebec Identity: The Challenge of Pluralism*. Trans. by Peter Feldstein. Montreal: McGill-Queen's University Press, 2003.

Masci, M. and E. Semino. "Politics Is Football: Metaphor in the Discourse of Silvio Berlusconi in Italy." *Discourse and Society* 7, no. 2 (1996): 243-69.

May, Steven. "Language and Education Rights for Indigenous Peoples," *Language, Culture and Curriculum* 11, no. 3 (1998): 272-296.

———. "Uncommon Languages: The Challenges and Possibilities of Minority Language Rights," *Journal of Multilingual and Multicultural Development* 21, no. 5 (2000): 366-385.

———. *Language and Minority Rights*. Harlow: Longman, 2001.

Milroy, James and Lesley Milroy. *Authority in Language: Investigating Language Prescription and Standardization*. London and Boston: Routledge & Kegan Paul, 1985.

Muyard, Frank. "From a Two-Chinas situation to a Taiwanese Nation in the Making: Democracy, Nationalism and the US Factor in the Transformation of Taiwan's "National" Identity," Paper presented at the Second Conference of the European Association of Taiwan Studies, Ruhr-Universitaet Bochum, Germany, April 1-2 2005.

Myers-Scotton, Carol. "The Possibility of Codeswitching: Motivation for Maintaining Multilingualism." *Anthropological Linguistics*, 14 (1972): 432-44.

———. "Strategies of Neutrality: Language Choice in Uncertain Situations," *Language* 52 (4) (1976): 919-941.

———. "The Negotiation of Identities in Conversation: A Theory of Markedness and Code Choice," *International Journal of Sociology of Language*, 44 (1983): 115-136.

———. *Social Motivations for Codeswitching: Evidence from Africa*. Oxford: Clarendon Press, 1993.

———. "A Theoretical Introduction to the Markedness Model." Pp. 18-38 in *Codes and Consequences: Choosing Linguistic Varieties*, edited by C. Myers-Scotton, New York: Oxford University Press, 1998.

———. "Explaining the Role of Norms and Rationality in Codeswitching," *Journal of Pragmatics* 32 (1999): 1259-1271.

Myers-Scotton, Carol and Agnes Bolonyai. "Calculating Speakers: Codeswitching in a Rational Choice Model." *Language in Society* 30, (2001): 1-28.

Myers-Scotton, Carol and William Ury. "Bilingual Strategies: The Social Functions of Codeswitching," *International Journal of Sociology of Language*, (1977): 5-20.

———. *Social Motivations for Codeswitching: Evidence from Africa*. Oxford: Clarendon Press, 1993b.

———. "Code-switching." Pp. 217-237 in *Handbook of Sociolinguistics*, edited by Florian Coulmias. Oxford: Blackwell, 1997a.

Norman, Jerry. *Chinese*. Cambridge and New York: Cambridge University Press, 1988.

Obeng, S. "Language and Politics: Indirectness in Political Discourse." *Language and Society*, 8(1) (1997): 49-83.

Patten, Alan. "Liberal Neutrality and Language Policy," *Philosophy & Public Affairs* 31, no. 4(2003): 356-386. Princeton University Press.

Price, Gareth. "The Language Barrier? Analyzing English Education in Taiwan." Paper presentation at the Second Conference of the European Association of Taiwan Studies. Ruhr University, Bochum. April 1-2, 2005.

Rabinow, Paul. *Reflections on Fieldwork in Morocco*. Berkeley: University of California Press, 1977.

Ramsey, S. Robert. *The Languages of China*. Princeton: Princeton University Press, 1987.

Rigger, Shelley. "Competing Conceptions of Taiwan's Identity: The Irresolvable Conflict in Cross-strait Relations," *Journal of Contemporary China* 6, Issue 15. July 1997.

———. *Politics in Taiwan: Voting For Democracy*. New York: Routledge, 1999.

Saussure, Ferdinand de. *Course in General Linguistics*. New York: Mcgraw-Hill, 1966.

Schmidt, Ronald, Sr. *Language Policy and Identity politics in the United States.* Temple University Press, 2000.

Scott, Mandy and Tiun, "Hak-Khiam Mandarin-only to Mandarin-plus: Taiwan." *Language Policy* (2007) 6:53-72.

Shih, Cheng-Feng. "Language and Ethnic Politics in Taiwan." Paper presented at the International Conference on Globalization, Education and Language. Department of English, College of Foreign Languages and Literatures, Tamkang University, Tamsui, Taiwan, November 15-16, 2002.

———. "A Chapter for the Aboriginals in the New Taiwan Constitution," [Taiwan xinxien zhong de yuanzhuminzu zhuanzhang]. Available at http://mail.tku.edu.tw/cfshih/seminar/20040722/html. 2004.

Shih, Cheng-feng, Bu-hsing Dali and Shih-kai Hsu. *"Aboriginal Autonomy and Rights."* [Yuanzhumin renchuan yu zizhi]. Taipei: Qienwei Publishing, 2001.

Shih, Y. H. "Socio-pragmatic Motivations for Code-switching in Taiwan." A research project report for National Science Council, Taiwan, 1995.

———. "The Socio-pragmatic Functions of Code-switching in Taiwan." Pp. 433-452 in *Proceedings of the Conference on Languages and Language Teaching in Taiwan.* National Hsinchu Teacher's College, 1998.

Shih, Y. H. and Z. Z. Su. "A Study of Mandarin Code-mixing in Taiwanese Speech." Paper presented at the First International Symposium on Languages in Taiwan, and then collected in *The Proceedings of the Symposium* (1995), pp. 731-767. Taipei: The Crane Publishing Co., Ltd., 1993.

Shih, Y. H. and M. H. Sung, (1998). "Code-mixing of Taiwanese in Mandarin Newspaper Headlines: A Socio-pragmatic Perspective." Pp. 46-74 in *The Proceedings of the Second International Symposium on Languages in Taiwan.* Taipei: The Crane Publishing Co., Ltd., 1998.

Simon, Scott. "Taiwan's Indigenized Constitution: What Place for Aboriginal Formosa?" Paper presented at the Second Conference of the European Association of Taiwan Studies, Ruhr-Universitaet Bochum, Germany, April 1-2, 2005.

Smith, Anthony. *National Identity.* Reno: University of Nevada Press, 1993.

Smith, Dennis. "Strategies for Multiculturalism: The Catalan Case Considered. A Response to Miquel Strubell," *Current Issues in Language and Society* 5, no. 3 (1998): 215-217.

Spence, Jonathan. *In Search of Modern China.* New York and London: W.W. Norton & Company, 1990.

Stroud, Christopher. "The Problem of Intention and Meaning in Codeswitching," *Text12* (1)(1992), Pp. 127-155.

Tannen, D. *Talking Voices: Repetition, Dialogue, and Imagery in Conversational Discourse.* Cambridge: Cambridge University Press, 1989.

Taylor, Charles. "Multiculturalism and 'The Politics of Recognition': An Essay by Charles Taylor." Princeton, New Jersey: Princeton University Press, 1992.

Tennessen, Carol. *Authority and Resistance in Language: From Michel Foucault to Compere Lapin.* Ann Arbor: University Microfilms International, 1985.

Bibliography

Tiu, H. "Writing in Two Scripts: A Case Study or Digraphia in Taiwanese." *Written Language and Literacy* 2, (1998): 225-247.

Tse, John Kwock-Ping. "Language and a Rising New Identity in Taiwan," *International Journal of Sociology of Language.* 143 (2000): 151-164.

———. "Language in Education and Language Planning in Taiwan: Recent Development." Paper presented at the Second International Symposium on Bilingualism in Chinese-speaking Communities. Hong Kong: University of Hong Kong, December 27-28, 2001.

Tu, Wei-ming. "The Living Tree: The Changing Meaning of Being Chinese Today." Edited by Tu Wei-ming. Stanford, CA: Stanford University Press. 1994

———. "Cultural China: The Periphery as the Center." Pp. 1-17 in *The Living Tree: The Changing Meaning of Being Chinese Today*, edited by Tu Wei-ming. Stanford: Stanford University Press, 1994.

Urciuoli, Bonnie. "Bilingualism as Code and Bilingualism as Practice." *Anthropological Linguistics* 27 (4)(1985): 363-86.

Voloshinov, V. N. *Marxism and the Philosophy of Language.* Cambridge: Harvard University Press, 1986.

Vygotsky, L. S. *Mind in Society: The Development of Higher Psychological Processes.* Cambridge, MA: Harvard University Press, 1978.

Wachman, Alan M. *Taiwan: National Identity and Democratization.* New York: M. E. Sharpe, 1994.

Wachman, Allen. "Competing Identities in Taiwan." Pp. 17-80 in *The Other Taiwan: 1945 to the Present*, Edited by Murray A. Rubinstein. Armonk, New York: M.E. Sharpe, 1994a.

———. *Taiwan: National Identity and Democratization.* New York: M.E. Sharpe, 1994b.

Wang, J. M. "The Sociopsychological Functions of Code-switching: A Case Study of the Presidential Campaign in Taiwan." Unpublished MA thesis. Fu Jen Catholic University, 2001.

Wang, Q. S. "A Survey of People's Attitudes Toward Youths' Adoption of Codeswitching." An unpublished manuscript, National Taiwan Normal University, 2003.

Wang, T. Y. "One China, One Taiwan: An Analysis of the Democratic Progressive Party's China Policy," Journal of Asian & African Studies (Brill) 35, Issue 1, 2000.

Wei, Jennifer M. Y. *Virtual Missiles: Allusions and Metaphors in Taiwanese Poilitical Campaigns.* Maryland, USA: Lexington Books, 2001a.

———. "Politeness and Politics: Chen Shui-bian's Rhetorical Strategies," *Journal of Humanities, National Cheng-Chi University* 83, (2001b): 1-23.

———. "Codeswitching in Campaigning Discourse: The Case of Taiwanese President Chen Shui-bian." *Journal of Language and Linguistics,* Academia Sinica, Taipei, Taiwan, 2002.

Weller, Robert P. "Religion and New Taiwanese Identities: Some First Thoughts," Harvard Studies on Taiwan, Paper of the Taiwan Studies Workshop, Vol. 3, 2000.

Wodak and Meyer eds. *Methods of Critical Discourse Analysis.* London: Sage

Publications, 2001.

Wright, Sue. "Reconciling Inclusion, Multiculturalism and Multilingualism," *Current Issues in Language and Society* 4, no. 2 (1997): 91-93.

———. *Language Policy and Language Planning: From Nationalism to Globalization*. New York: Palgrave Macmillan, 2004.

Wu, David Yen-ho. "The Construction of Chinese and Non-Chinese Identities." Pp. 148-167 in *The Living Tree: The Changing Meaning of Being Chinese Today*, edited by Tu Wei-ming. Stanford: Stanford University Press, 1994.

Yeh, His-nan, Hui-chen Chan, and Yuh-show Cheng. "Language Use in Taiwan: Language Proficiency and Domain Analysis," *Journal of Taiwan Normal University Humanities & Social Sciences*, 2004, 49 (1), 75-107.

Zhang, Wei. "Code-choice in Bidialectal Interaction: The Choice between Putonghua and Cantonese in a Radio Phone-in Program in Shenzhen." *Journal of Pragmatics* 37 (2005): 355–374.

Zhang, Qing. "A Chinese Yuppie in Beijing: Phonological Variation and the Construction of a New Professional Identity." *Language in Society* 34:3 (2005) 431–466.

Index

2/28 Incident, 10, 47, 53n8, 59–60

Benshengren, 63, 65, 78n10

Chen Shui-bian, 26, 29, 32–34, 39–40, 51, 105
Chinese: Chinese language, 4, 7, 16n2, 78n6, 92, 111, 116; Chinese people, 93
codeswitching, 19, 25, 33, 66, 69, 72, 105, 106

Democratic Progressive Party (DPP), 28, 39–42, 44–45, 47–48, 50–53, 55, 61, 64–67, 70–77, 79n15, 84, 94, 98–99, 105–106, 109–110, 117
dialogue(s), 12–13, 56, 66, 68, 72–74, 76
discourse, 4, 12–14, 16n2, 19, 28, 30, 51, 55, 62, 68–69, 81–83, 100, 104, 108, 112, 115, 118

globalization, 83–84, 86–88, 95, 104, 114, 118
Greater China, 103–104, 106–107, 110, 113–114, 116–117, 119, 119n1

identity, 1, 3–5, 11–16, 19–23, 26–27, 29––32, 35, 47, 51, 55–57, 59, 61–66, 68, 70, 72–75, 81–82, 86, 91, 94, 96–97, 100, 103–104, 106–119
identity politics, 1, 56, 61, 64, 73, 76, 82, 109, 115–119
indigenization, 65, 86, 88, 97, 104, 114
indirectness, 26–27, 34

Kuomintang (KMT), 1, 17n18, 20–24, 37–46, 50–51, 52n2, 53n6n10n13, 55–67, 70–76, 83, 85, 88, 91–100, 100n7, 105–106, 108–110, 115, 117

language choice, 19, 25, 30–31, 32n1, 33–34, 37, 52, 56, 59, 65–69, 71–72, 74–77, 79n17, 82, 84, 88, 106, 113–114, 116
language policy, 7, 20–22, 30, 40, 47, 52, 56–57, 61, 67, 77, 81–86, 88, 91, 93, 95, 97–99, 116

Mandarin, 2–8, 11–15, 17n17, 19–32, 37–53, 55–59, 61, 65–68, 70–77, 77n1, 78n6, 79n14n17, 81–85, 87–90, 92–95, 97–99, 103–106, 108, 111–116
multiculturalism, 77, 81–84, 88, 97–100, 111, 113, 115

nationalism, 2, 9, 15, 38, 52n1, 57, 61–63, 74, 76, 81, 86, 91–93, 98–100, 107–109, 113, 115–116, 118

political discourse, 22, 25–27, 29, 31, 33–34, 36, 51, 64, 68–69, 105, 115–116
Putonghua, 5, 7, 9, 13–14, 31, 92

Rational Choice model (RC), 19, 28, 33–34, 43, 51, 71, 105

Taiwanese language, 93
Tai-yu, 1, 6–7, 9, 16n10, 19–33, 37–52, 53n5, 55–58, 61, 65–77, 77n1,

79n14n15n17, 85, 87, 89, 92, 94–95, 98–99, 103, 105–106, 108, 111–116, 120

translinguistic(s), 2–3, 12, 56, 68–69, 72–74, 76

voice, 12–13, 27, 41, 56, 69, 72–76, 82, 94, 99, 112, 115

Waishengren, 51, 63, 65, 78n10

About the Author

Jennifer M. Wei is professor of English at Soochow University, Taipei, Taiwan and has served as department chairperson (2004-2007). For 2008 she is also a visiting professor in the Queens College Department of Classic, Middle Eastern and Asian Languages and Cultures and a visiting scholar at the Chinese Studies Center at Berkeley. Her recent publications include two books published by Lexington Books, a division of Rowman & Littlefield Publishers—*Virtual Missiles: Allusions and Metaphors Used in Taiwanese Political Discourse* (2001) and *Language Choice and Identity Politics in Taiwan* (2008). Both were made possible by grants from the Chiang Ching-kuo International Scholarly Foundation.